The
THATCHER
YEARS
Britain and Latin America

Latin America Bureau

First published in Great Britain in 1988 by
Latin America Bureau (Research and Action) Limited
1 Amwell Street
London EC1R 1UL

British Library Cataloguing in Publication Data

The Thatcher years: Britain and Latin America
  1. Great Britain – Foreign relations – Latin America
  2. Latin America – Foreign relations – Great Britain
  3. Great Britain – Foreign relations – 1945–
  4. Latin America – Foreign relations – 1948–
  I. Ferguson, James II. Pearce, Jenny
  327.4108 D A 47.9.L29

  ISBN 0 906156 38 6

Edited by James Ferguson and Jenny Pearce
Additional material by Debbie MacDonald and Duncan Green

The views expressed by contributors are not necessarily those of the
Latin America Bureau

Cover illustration © Kevin Kallaugher
Cover design by Jan Brown
Trade distribution by Third World Publications, 151 Stratford Road,
Birmingham B11 1RD

Typeset, printed and bound by Calvert's Press, London

Contents

Contributors

Jon Barnes, former National Secretary, Chile Committee for Human Rights, is on the staff of *Socialist Affairs*.

Jimmy Burns is on the staff of the *Financial Times* and is the author of *The Land That Lost Its Heroes: The Falklands, The Post War and Alfonsín* (Bloomsbury, 1987).

James Ferguson is a writer/researcher at the Latin America Bureau.

Judith Hart is a former Labour Minister for Overseas Development.

Hugh O'Shaughnessy is the Latin America correspondent for the *Observer*.

James Painter is a writer/researcher at the Latin America Bureau.

Jenny Pearce is a writer/researcher at the Latin America Bureau.

John Tanner is a freelance journalist, specialising in development issues.

Preface

Successive British governments have made fundamental blunders in their attitudes towards Latin America. In particular, they have consistently underestimated the region's importance for Britain. But there is a good argument that this is merely the most recent of a series of strategic misjudgments which have dogged British foreign policy since the end of the Second World War.

As that war came to an end, politicians and civil servants were understandably ruled by twin obsessions. On the one hand, there was the need to prepare for an eventual retreat from Britain's increasingly impossible position as an imperial power – a retreat which was carried out with more success than could ever have been expected. On the other, was the need to maintain a so called 'special relationship' with the United States, the most powerful country in the world at that time.

However, these obsessions completely overshadowed the issue of Britain's relationship with Europe, and the need for an enfeebled Britain to seek strength through a commitment to its European neighbours. When entry to the European Community was finally achieved, Britain seemed thankful to turn its back on entanglements in the developing countries of the Commonwealth and the rest of what was now called the 'Third World'. Instead, it threw itself enthusiastically into the game of flirting simultaneously in Brussels and Washington. The markets of the Commonwealth and the investment opportunities there could not compete with those in the United States and the Community. The rest of the world, apart from the Soviet Union, Japan and possibly China, was seen as comparatively marginal, worthy of the attention of neither the established policy makers nor those bidding for power. Latin America, an area where Britain had once been economically pre-eminent, hardly figured in policy planning.

The arrival in Downing Street in 1979 of a Prime Minister with little experience of, or interest in, international relations did nothing to change the accepted wisdom. In the first few months of her premiership, it took Lord Carrington as Foreign and Commonwealth Secretary to initiate Mrs Thatcher into the intricacies of foreign affairs and persuade her of the perils of following her instincts and doing a deal with the illegal white Rhodesian regime.

The Falklands war of 1982 was the point where Latin America forced itself into the forefront of the British political agenda for the first time since the early years of the last century. The fact that that war ended well for the British government – and indeed assisted in the re-election of Mrs Thatcher – should not be allowed to obscure the many errors and omissions which, combined with Argentine military triumphalism, helped bring it about. The over-concentration by the British government on relationships with Europe and the United States meant that intelligence from the region was bad and that what little there was did not reach the higher levels of government.

General Galtieri was convinced he had little to fear from Margaret Thatcher. Her clear sympathy for the military regimes of Chile and Argentina was revealed by the ministerial visits of such favourites as Mr Peter Rees and Mr Cecil Parkinson, and the absence of effective official criticism of the human rights violations in those countries. Ships of the Argentine navy had been on exercise in Cardigan Bay only days before the invasion of the islands without eliciting any official response.

The decisions by the Thatcher government in late 1981 to maintain the garrison on the Falklands at derisory levels and to scrap HMS *Endurance*, the ice patrol vessel of the Royal Navy in the Antarctic, were taken as part of a long series of signals from Britain to Argentina that nobody in Whitehall cared about the Falklands.

The last minute incompetence of the Thatcher government in the months leading up to the invasion was the fruit of long established neglect. It was to cost the two countries hundreds of lives and billions of pounds worth of revenue. It is a measure of the great political talents of the Prime Minister that she engineered the recapture of the islands in a way which won the support of the majority of people in Britain who had perhaps not grasped the government's responsibility for the original invasion. Today, despite the massive expenditure on defence in the South Atlantic, British prestige is still a hostage to the whim of any ultra-nationalist Argentine officer who takes it into his head to destroy the precarious peace in the South Atlantic by attacking the British.

British neglect of the Third World in general, and Latin America in particular, has also led to large losses for the British Exchequer. Latin America owes the rest of the world US$400 billion and poses serious problems for British banks as a result of the debt crisis. This crisis could yet test the very foundations of the international financial system. The 'big four' British clearing banks are variously estimated to have between £13 billion and £20 billion out in loans to Latin America. The most exposed and weakest of the four, Midland, is calculated to have committed no less than 185 per cent of its shareholders' funds to the region as a result of its headlong and inexpert sweep into Latin American lending in the 1970s.

The weakness of British banks in Latin America has been clear for several years. The British government has insisted, however, on the theory that market forces were to be as paramount in international affairs as they were supposed to be in the British economy. This has meant that years were lost in the search for effective international co-operation between exposed lenders and overloaded borrowers following the crisis which broke out in Mexico in 1982. This delay has in its turn led the Exchequer to suffer losses as British banks are forced to make big provision for the bad debts they have contracted in Latin America and thereby reduce their tax liabilities. In September 1987, Mr Nigel Lawson, the Chancellor, put the loss to the Treasury at one billion pounds.

The Thatcher government, which all along has insisted that the debt crisis should not involve government action, has had to face the fact that in common with other creditor governments, it is being forced to the international bargaining table. The debt crisis has proved to be too big for even the most ambitious of the commercial banks' 'co-ordinating committees' to tackle. The debtors' argument that the crisis must be alleviated by government action has prevailed. They have announced that they are abandoning the prescriptions of austerity advanced by the creditors and are now unwilling and unable to service their liabilities.

It is interesting to note that a demoralised British manufacturing sector has not in general made its voice heard in the debate on economic relations with Latin America. The continuing loss of British manufacturing exports to the region has come about without great complaint from British industrialists. They have failed to point out the losses to this country of considerable visible trade due to the region's financial plight and the unwillingness of the international financial community to heed Latin America's calls for the opportunity of economic growth.

As with the Falklands, the result of the debt crisis has been disorder and loss for Britain, together with the persistence of an international threat. It could justifiably be argued that the threats faced by the British banks from Latin American debtors, and the threats to Britain's credibility as a military power from Argentina, are more serious and immediate than any others the Thatcher government has had to deal with.

Given the persistence in London of the conviction that Britain has the secret of squaring the circle, and can maintain as close links with the US government as with our fellow members of the European Community, it would be unwise to expect any initiative from the Thatcher government which might improve relations with Latin America.

As a fellow conservative and a valued counsellor of President Ronald Reagan, Mrs Thatcher has been particularly unwilling to criticise his support for terrorism in Central America. She has kept silent on Central America publicly and, one suspects, privately. This is despite the fact that the immediate interest of Britain with its large garrison of troops permanently stationed on Central American soil in Belize, must be for a political not military solution to the crisis in the isthmus. Arms for the terrorists operating in Nicaragua have been contracted and forwarded from Britain, often, it should be remembered, from countries such as Yugoslavia and Poland. A private 'security' company which has provided many bodyguards at British embassies abroad, has, on the evidence of Lieutenant-Colonel Oliver North, been implicated in the sabotage of installations in Nicaragua. Yet even where the government's own enquiries have revealed law-breaking in Britain by the supporters of the Central American terrorists, as in the case of the *Silver Sea* (the arms ship which sailed illegally from Southampton in February 1986), Whitehall has refused to prosecute. Had those engaged in trying to destroy the Nicaraguan government from Britain instead involved themselves in sabotaging the oil installations at Rotterdam rather than Corinto or planted bombs in Milan rather than Managua, the reaction in London would surely have been different.

British participation in the Community Foreign Ministers' consultations with their Central American counterparts in San José, Luxembourg and Guatemala has been grudging. An eye has always been kept on Washington's sensitivities about any major European demarches in the isthmus. And, as the *Observer* chronicled at the time, British officials have, in a way the Reagan administration must have applauded, sought any excuse or none to block funds from international financial agencies to the government of Nicaragua. At the same time, Britain has provided token military training at the Royal Military Academy, Sandhurst, to the forces of El Salvador. The move is reminiscent of that time when, in another gaffe doubtless attributable to the same low level of diplomatic oversight traditionally employed on Central America, the doors of that institution were opened to the Somoza family.

The policies of the government towards Central America have, however, had to be executed in a virtually clandestine manner, so unpopular would they have been had they been exposed to greater public scrutiny. At the level of the intelligent citizen interested in foreign affairs, there has been a growing awareness of the horrors of Central America following on those of Brazil in the 1960s and 1970s, Chile since 1973 and Argentina under the generals. While the politicians and diplomats have weaved and tacked, public opinion has had a very clear idea of the issues and moral values at stake. Officials at the Foreign and Commonwealth Office have at times complained that Central America has prompted more letters of public concern than any other foreign policy issue. Such concern is a measure of the efforts of the Central American lobby in Britain, which numbers some very eminent members of the establishment among its activists. It also clearly draws on a well of spontaneous popular outrage over events in the isthmus.

How British relations with Latin America will continue to be handled during the rest of Mrs Thatcher's premiership cannot be accurately foreseen. It is likely, however, that the pressure from the debtor nations will gradually force easier repayment terms out of Britain and the other major lenders, and that public funds will be available in the last instance if there is any risk of failure by a major British bank. A tiny community of fewer than 2,000 people in the Falkland Islands, grown increasingly affluent on the revenues from fishing, will surely become more politically conscious and articulate about their interests. The solution of the dispute with Argentina over the islands will consequently become more complicated, though not impossible.

At home, the increasing ease of travel and availability of news will, it must be hoped, stimulate the public's appetite for better and more perceptive British policies towards the region.

1. A 'special relationship'

The last twenty years have seen startling developments in British political attitudes towards Latin America. Twenty years ago we were, frankly, not very interested and even less involved (except for a few specialist academics and journalists). There were some nasty dictatorships, we knew. But Latin America was part of the US sphere of influence, wasn't it? We had our own concerns in Africa: Rhodesia and UDI; the struggle for independence of the Portuguese colonies in Africa; the evils of apartheid in South Africa. These were matters of direct post-colonial British concern, and absorbed some of the energies of the minority of activists involved in international issues. To be sure, Cuba had aroused our anxieties, but that was in part because we trembled in terror on the brink of nuclear war as Kennedy and Khruschev confronted each other. Peace and nuclear disarmament were the issues of the 1960s, leading directly to the passionate commitment of so many to campaigning against the war in Vietnam. These concerns dominated our own foreign policy debate between and within the political parties into the early 1970s.

Twenty years is so short a time in history. But in this fast moving century, they can witness massive changes in relationships between countries and peoples. In 1967, the European Community was something happening across the Channel, but not to us. 'Third World' was a phrase which was only just being invented. Third World debt was being accumulated, but no one was worried, least of all the banks. Television carried no programmes about Latin America. Newspapers and weeklies carried very little. It was a long time ago.

There were, of course, plenty of solid British relationships with the countries of South America and the Caribbean. Trading and financial links were strong and thriving, and the thrust of Foreign Office diplomatic effort was to encourage them. Parliamentary backbench interest was largely limited to Conservative members with business interests in Brazil, Chile, Argentina, or wherever. Britain, after all, had long connections there. Read a novel written in the 1920s or 1930s: the black sheep of the family, or the adventurer, or the rugged hero with a secret past – Argentina was their habitat. Hear the story one is told in Peru (not that I believe it), that the reason Peruvian men and women peasants wear their hard black hats is that they admired the bowlers worn by the British who came out to plan the

Pacific coast railway. There had been the British colonial adventures, which left us still with Guyana and Belize and most of the islands of the Caribbean. These dependencies were moving during the 1960s into independence or the elaborate compromise of Associated Statehood. The British public was far less interested in their constitutional status or their political and economic problems than in how many of their people should be allowed to be immigrants to Britain.

From Allende to Pinochet

The catalyst for a change of political attitude was, without question, the election of a marxist, socialist government in Chile and the military coup which ended it and murdered President Allende on 11 September 1973. The 'Chilean experiment' excited interest on the left. For here was one of the only Latin American democracies (established as long ago as 1834) electing its *Unidad Popular* (Popular Unity) government, based on an alliance of Allende's Socialist Party, the Communist Party, the left Christian Democrats, the Radical Party (affiliated, like the British Labour Party, to the Socialist International), and two other minor socialist parties. Would it succeed? What would it do? It was, we perceived, the very first democratically elected government in the world to call its approach marxist. There was no intense mass interest on the part of the British or European labour movement, but there was enough to stimulate the Bureau of the Socialist International to hold one of its regular meetings, at considerable expense, in Santiago in March 1973 to give support to Popular Unity in its municipal elections that month. The Socialist International, frankly, carries little weight in Western Europe, where socialist parties have far more on their minds than the resolutions of the last Bureau meeting. But in Latin America and the Caribbean, its endorsements and its pronouncements count for a great deal to the democratic socialist parties struggling for survival and for power.

By now, the IMF and the World Bank and, through its dominant controlling interest, Washington, were fiercely resisting the economic and social policies of the Chilean government. That government's land reform measures – which were hated not only because they were so radical, but because they were effective – dispossessed the rich landowners. Its transfer to public ownership of key industries (including copper) meant the expropriation of the industrial and financial interests of some of the most powerful US-based multinational corporations. The alliance of the State Department with Kennecott (the copper barons), ITT and the CIA, whose anti-Allende conspiracies are all too well documented, presented a threat to the *Unidad Popular* savage enough, in the end, to overwhelm it.

Where Washington led, London followed. The years of Allende were precisely the years of the Heath Conservative government. We cannot know until the files are opened in the first years of the 21st century whether British policy towards Chile was the subject of Cabinet or Cabinet Committee reporting and deliberation, or whether it was one of those many areas of foreign policy where officials assume, and Foreign Secretaries endorse, maximum agreement and co-operation with the United States, without regarding it as necessary to consult Cabinet colleagues. Certainly, Sir Alec Douglas Home at his Foreign Office desk could take it for granted that he had the full support of Conservative backbenchers and *The Times* in sharp hostility to the Chilean government. They labelled it 'communist', despite the fact that within it the Communist Party was the moderating, 'take it gently and consolidate' influence, and the non-communist socialist party of Allende himself was forcing the pace of socialist advance. For the British Conservative Party, Chile had been the Latin American country whose navy Britain trained and most of whose naval ships we supplied; where our trading, commercial and banking interests were with the very companies plotting subversion; where British Council money was largely concentrated on assisting a large private school for the upper class in Santiago; and where the British ambassador's cocktail party guests and friends were entirely 'the Mercurio crowd'. This is my own label for the bitterly anti-government business people and journalists who graced the ambassador's drawing room and his dinner table, all of them in perfect harmony with the right wing views of *El Mercurio*, which were faithfully reflected in the leader columns of the pre-Murdoch *Times*.

What became absolutely clear, before and after the 1973 military coup, was that Washington and London cared nothing for democracy in their passion to oppose socialism in Latin America. Britain, to put it at the very least, acquiesced in the US conspiracy to overthrow Allende.

But the events of September 1973 produced a strong reaction from the labour movement in Britain. The first Trafalgar Square protest – which was big – was followed by the creation of the Chile Solidarity Campaign, the first of the solidarity groups of the 1970s and 1980s concerned with Latin and Central America. It emerged out of party conference statements and resolutions, a Labour promoted debate in the House of Commons, and a deep and very real grass roots concern. It mobilised strong and committed trade union support. For the first time, Latin America was on the foreign policy agenda in Britain.

In the five years that followed the election of a Labour government in 1974, official aid to Chile was stopped, to be replaced by the channelling of modest funds (some £3 million) through the voluntary agencies to help the poor and oppressed in Chile, bypassing Pinochet's regime. Refugees were admitted, and Home Office help given to organisations helping them to settle here. Refugees came not only from Chile, but from other countries such as Argentina and Uruguay. Arms sales were ended (though there were problems about one or two legally-binding contracts, which the trade unions resolved by shop-floor action). Protests were made about torture, imprisonments and killings. World Bank loans were opposed, sometimes with success, sometimes not. In the United States, President Carter, rarely given credit for it, embarked upon a serious campaign about human rights in Latin America.

But under Nixon, the IMF and the World Bank had rushed to the rescue of the Chilean economy, thoroughly approving of Pinochet's reliance on the advice of Milton Friedman's 'Chicago Boys'. That their economic prescription resulted in 30 per cent unemployment by the 1980s, and in desperate poverty for so many, was neither here nor there to Margaret Thatcher when she came to power in 1979. She liked the economic philosophy of the Chicago Boys.

1979: a new direction

The Heath government's policy towards Chile may have been casual, a mere endorsement of Washington's approach. But one is bound to conclude that the Thatcher government took conscious and deliberate policy decisions. Almost at once, in spite of protests, pleas, and a Labour frontbench delegation to see him, the Home Secretary, William Whitelaw, abandoned the Latin American refugee programme, which had helped many Chileans and fugitives from other harsh military dictatorships. Roughly coinciding with Reagan's election as President, arms sales resumed and British training of naval and other military personnel, modest in numbers but important in principle, was begun again. The reversal of Labour government policies was too early and too decisive to reflect any personal persuasions from Reagan: the very special relationship between him and Mrs Thatcher was still gestating. No doubt there were Washington pressures, but the policy switch was essentially British.

Chile was the catalyst in the 1970s for the involvement in Latin American issues of the left in Britain, and, indeed, Europe. Our campaigning here was fully matched in France, Italy, Germany and the Nordic countries, and refugees were scattered across the continent, from Glasgow to Moscow. The 1980s have produced new issues in plenty.

The Falklands/Malvinas question had been gently simmering away for many years, and the history of it is now well enough known. What was extraordinary and unforgivable was that Mrs Thatcher, the Conservative government and the Tory Party (there were a few honourable exceptions) discovered by some kind of divine revelation that General Galtieri was a particularly nasty military dictator only after the invasion of the Falklands. The months which preceded it had seen trade delegations and the usual currency of diplomatic courtesies. During the years before it, those concerned for human rights had sought to help the persecuted to escape from Argentine prisons to sanctuary in Britain. For 'fascist' Argentina had a strange policy which allowed a political prisoner his or her release if entry to a host country was guaranteed and signed on the dotted line. Trade unions had 'adopted' prisoners or individuals in danger of arrest or – perhaps more likely – 'disappeared'. Thus, for example, Equity gave a precious membership card to a young Argentine actress who had devoted herself to literacy work among the peasants of Argentina, and, in danger, managed to escape to Britain. Amnesty International had named Argentine 'prisoners of conscience', and there was awareness and concern about the many thousands of the 'disappeared'. The atrocities which led eventually to the trials, under President Alfonsín, of the generals and officers responsible were well documented. But Mrs Thatcher did not want to know – until the invasion of the Falklands.

At that moment, Mrs Thatcher's Latin American policies took her into a closer relationship with Pinochet in Chile, and with Reagan in Washington. Chile had its own territorial dispute with Argentina (the Beagle Channel), and was a natural and, on occasion, very useful ally in the Falklands war. Reagan provided modest but important support, particularly in the field of intelligence information, and in accepting and sustaining Mrs Thatcher's reluctance to seek a negotiated solution. It is since the end of the war that she has paid her political debts to Reagan. To have done so, however, will not have disturbed her sleep, for her own thinking runs so close to his. In foreign policy, they are birds of a feather.

Loyalty to Washington

Three countries which have prompted demonstrations of solidarity with Washington are, of course, Nicaragua, Grenada and Jamaica.

The overthrow of the Somoza regime in Nicaragua and its replacement by the Sandinistas took place at a time when the military dictatorships of Latin America were crumbling one by one. They fell in Argentina, Peru, Brazil, Uruguay, to be replaced by delicately poised and tender democracies. With the decay of the dictatorships, US hegemony was at an end. These were countries with memories of US support for the generals, and with economic problems which eventually led them into some degree of confrontation with US commercial and financial interests. For the combination of oil price rises, high interest rates and lower commodity prices had brought each of them to regard the problem of their debts, owed mainly to US banks, as by far the most serious confronting them. They found the 'adjustment' formulae imposed by the IMF as conditions for assistance and debt rescheduling impossible to accept. The reforms and restructuring eagerly expected by peoples newly liberated from right-wing oppression could not be delivered in times of such desperate economic difficulty. The debt crisis has threatened not only their financial viability but the survival of their newly found democracy. And the enemy was North American: the banks, the IMF and Washington's support for both.

Central America and the Caribbean became far more important for the State Department and the Pentagon. The USA's back door had at all costs to be protected from the Russians and the Cubans and all the other 'commie' threats. No matter that there was a vocal body of US opinion which opposed the policies pursued agaist the government of Nicaragua (duly democratically elected). No matter that it included many leading men of the churches. No matter that US naval intervention – mining the ports – was condemned and declared unlawful by the International Court of Justice. The saga of the funding of the contras, CIA activity, the mobilisation of support from Honduras and El Salvador, and opposition to World Bank loans continued through the years until Irangate – and, if Reagan has his way, beyond Irangate.

In articulating British reaction to all this, the Foreign Office has had a very difficult time indeed. Given the size of the Conservative majority in the House of Commons, neither Mrs Thatcher nor Sir Geoffrey Howe have needed to worry too much about questions and criticisms from the Opposition. Nor would Mrs Thatcher ever worry about the campaign for Nicaragua in the towns and cities of Britain, strongly mobilised as it is. If the City and the CBI and the Tory Party are content, she is undisturbed. But the European Community is another kettle of fish. It would not be at all prudent or appropriate, to use two favourite Foreign Office words, for Britain to veto an EEC statement which accepted a ruling of the International Court of Justice; or to be the only EEC member country to resist a call for increased aid to Nicaragua in its US-provoked distress.

So it is that we have watched Sir Geoffrey walk a tightrope. In the most muted tones that even he can command, he has endorsed EEC pronouncements – about aid, about the mining of ships, about the International Court of Justice, and about the need to support the earlier efforts of the Contadora Group to find a negotiated solution. But he has done so only under pressure. There seem to have been no Foreign Office efforts to ensure that the media fully grasped their importance. They have been covered in the briefest possible sentence in statements he has made to Parliament following meetings of the EEC. And from Mrs Thatcher we have heard next to nothing. Her frequent discussions with Reagan have produced no public mention of Nicaragua, except to indicate her general sympathy with his problems. It is one of the prices she has paid – perhaps willingly enough – for his support in the Falklands war. The Irangate enquiries have indicated that the British market economy under Mrs Thatcher was able to permit the covert sale of arms to the contras. We shall probably never know how far she did or did not have direct discussions with Reagan's messengers about help for the contras, or what she said.

The EEC, of course, provides a useful safety net on many occasions when public protest must be answered, permitting a policy with two faces. One is the public face: quote EEC condemnations of the abuse of human rights in Chile and US actions against Nicaragua. The other is the private face: go on selling arms to Chile and block loans to Nicaragua and, maybe, do rather more than that.

Grenada: silent complicity

The Grenada issue could not be resolved by reference to the EEC. The New Jewel Movement which replaced a corrupt and despised government under Eric Gairy, was socialist; its leader, Maurice Bishop, was yet another marxist with democratic intentions. The Conservative government disliked it intensely. And there was another factor which was important. The New Jewel government established close relations with Cuba. When no other sources of finance were forthcoming, Cuba gave assistance to build Grenada's new airport, which Grenada needed, to share in the expansion of European and North American tourism in the Caribbean. And the conventional thinking in both London and Washington was that anyone who is a friend of Cuba is an enemy of ours.

The same principle governed attitudes to Jamaica, where Michael Manley's government during the 1970s established friendly detente with Cuba, its near neighbour, and with which it, like Grenada, shared membership of the Non-Aligned Movement. But comings and goings between Kingston, St George's and Havana alarmed Washington. When Reagan took office he launched his initiative to establish and secure US domination in the Caribbean. If Latin America was moving away from him, and Nicaragua was disturbing the security of his traditional backyard, the rest of the backyard had better be fenced in pretty firmly. Attention therefore focused on the Caribbean, which had been singularly unimportant for Carter, whose wife had paid an official friendly visit to Jamaica in Manley's years, and who showed no inclination to strengthen US economic or military influence as a perceived policy objective.

The field was wide open for Reagan. Initiatives taken by the British Labour government in 1978 and 1979 to stimulate a fresh approach to aid-supported economic co-operation in the Caribbean Basin, involving the World Bank, the EEC and the Latin American Caribbean states, with a limited degree of support from the State Department (it was lukewarm, but it participated) were quickly dropped when the Conservative government was elected. This was not at all surprising. The Foreign Office had been dismally unenthusiastic, finding the islands of the Caribbean both boring and unimportant to British interests, despite their membership of the Commonwealth. There was a political vacuum, which Reagan moved fast to fill. The essential aim of his economic initiative was to encourage and support private investment, although it has a very limited role to play in resolving the social and economic problems of the islands. His plans were supported by diplomatic efforts to consolidate extended economic links.

Events in Grenada played into his hands. Popular support for New Jewel's radical reforms, urgently needed after the years of neglect and near-gangsterism of Eric Gairy, was sharply threatened by a schism in the leadership and the party itself. Bernard Coard, who was Bishop's deputy, and a group which came to be known as the Coard faction, adopted an extreme marxist-leninist approach with strong direct links to Moscow. In the pre-Gorbachev era, Moscow exhibited every sign of infantile disorder and of total failure to understand the political realities of a tiny island with all its colonial inheritance of British traditions. Those traditions linger long after colonialism is dead, and this was only a very few years in the case of Grenada. The outcome was the attempted coup by the Coard group, and the terrible massacre of Maurice Bishop and many civilians. Just who was responsible for the murders and the shootings is still, at the time of writing, a matter for the courts and the legal process. But what is certain is that it was a terrible and traumatic experience for the people of Grenada.

It was an opportunity for Reagan. The invasion was accomplished with an efficiency that could only demonstrate very considerable intelligence information and careful pre-planning, and was immediately followed by the highly successful mobilisation of support from most of the countries of the Commonwealth Caribbean and the co-operation of the Governor-General of Grenada. To be sure, Trinidad and Guyana strongly dissented. To be sure, the Queen and the Secretary-General of the Commonwealth were deeply disturbed, and were deprived of information until the operation was complete and US forces had occupied Grenada. To be in Grenada some three months later was to see the full extent of that occupation and to note with interest that the US chargé d'affaires in Grenada was no less a person than the man who had been ambassador in Jamaica. A rather humbling diplomatic demotion in conventional career terms? Not in this case, clearly.

In all of this, Mrs Thatcher did and said next to nothing. For her, Grenada might have been a dot in outer space. Commonwealth responsibility and interest was of no consequence to her. The Queen's concern did not matter. The British Prime Minister acquiesced in the illegal US invasion of Grenada with scarcely a comment. In doing so, she endorsed the US assertion of its dominance over and strategic control of the Caribbean. British and Commonwealth international influence has never been yielded so cheaply.

In all the complexities of British relationships with Latin and Central America and the Caribbean in the last decade, the abdication of responsibility for or interest in Grenada is the clearest indication we have of a fundamental change in British foreign policy. This is now tailored to meet the exigencies of Mrs Thatcher's own perception of international priorities and her very special relationship with President Reagan. Perhaps the former was dominant in her earlier years, but now there is little to choose between them.

2. Private solutions: debt and development

The 1980s have brought Latin America's worst economic crisis for decades. This has meant very little or no growth, high levels of open unemployment, low levels of investment and foreign trade and, above all, increased poverty for the majority of its population. According to the 1987 report of the Inter-American Development Bank (IDB), for 13 out of 25 Latin American countries, per capita Gross Domestic Product (GDP) in 1986 was at least ten per cent lower than it was in 1980.

The debt crisis has played a major role in the creation of this tragic picture, and the response of the lender nations to the crisis has only deepened the region's problems. British banks have made millions of pounds from their lending to the continent, and the City of London is still heavily involved with Latin America. But the Thatcher government is imbued with the philosophy that the market must solve all economic ills. It has fully backed the IMF adjustment programmes whose main objective is to secure, by whatever means, continued interest payments by debtor governments to their creditors. But the effect of the programmes has not been to assist Latin American countries back on the path of economic growth.

It is the poorest people of Latin America who have borne the greatest burden of Thatcher/IMF strategies. Britain's aid programme to Latin America is just one example of how economic policies based on the 'magic of the market place' simply allow governments to ignore the plight of the world's poor and underprivileged.

The politics of aid

The British government's official 'overseas aid' to Latin America is very small. In 1986, gross bilateral (country to country) aid from the UK to the Americas was only £60 million out of a worldwide total of £847 million; a mere seven per cent. What is more, most of that marginal sum was allocated either to the Caribbean (£25 million) or to the Falklands/Malvinas (£10 million). Latin America does not have the population, the historical ties or the degree of poverty to attract larger amounts of aid.

Britain's attitude to the region is mirrored by the other Western industrial countries. 'ODA (official development assistance) to the Americas of the order of US$4.5 billion is relatively insignificant', says the OECD, the rich nations' club. Between 1984 and 1985 only 16.5 per cent of total bilateral aid went to Latin America and the Caribbean, for example, although Britain and other rich nations also provide aid to the region through their contributions to the World Bank, European Community aid and the UN agencies.

The main reason for the very low percentage of British aid is the policy of 'aid to the poorest', introduced by the former Labour Minister for Overseas Development, Judith Hart. Only Haiti is classified by the World Bank as a 'low income' country in Latin America. Despite obvious widespread poverty and inequality, most countries in Latin America and the Caribbean have relatively high levels of *average* Gross National Product (GNP) per person. Among Third World nations they rank as 'middle income' and not as the poorest. It remains true that only 15 in every 100 of the world's army of the hungry are people from Latin America or the Caribbean. In international terms the region is comparatively well off, even if living standards for most people remain far below those of North America, Europe or Japan.

According to the World Bank, 13 per cent of the region's people – 50 million individuals – do not get enough to eat. In 1980, they consumed fewer than 90 per cent of the calories deemed necessary by the World Health Organisation for an active working life. Bolivia, for example, which just scrapes into the category of middle income, recorded one of the highest levels of infant mortality in the world in 1985. One Bolivian child in every ten dies before reaching his or her first birthday, according to official figures.

In many countries, the recession of the early 1980s and the debt crisis deepened poverty. Even average living standards across the board in South America were 6.5 per cent below their 1980 level, reported the IDB in 1987. As noted in the introduction, the IDB drew particular attention to the dramatic fall in average GDP per person, especially in Bolivia, Guatemala, Guyana and Trinidad & Tobago. The poor of all countries have been badly affected by the economic crisis and their numbers increased. In Santiago, Chile, for example, malnutrition among school age children increased from 4.6 per cent in 1980 to 15.8 per cent in 1983. In Jamaica the numbers admitted to the main children's hospital suffering from malnutrition doubled between 1978 and 1985, reports UNICEF.

The degree of poverty 'should be assessed not by reference to per capita income alone, but by reference to the extent to which there are poor people within the country', concluded the House of Commons Foreign Affairs Committee, examining bilateral aid in 1987. But since 1980 the Conservative government has added three extra criteria to the maxim of aid to the poorest. According to Neil Marten MP, in a Commons debate of 1980, it gives 'greater weight in the allocation of our aid to political, industrial and commercial considerations alongside our basic development objective'.

It is these criteria which explain the lopsided allocation of overseas aid to Latin America and the Caribbean. Why else should Bolivians have received only 31p each in 1986, Jamaicans a mere £1.72 and the islanders of the Falklands/Malvinas as much as £5,000 per person?

The Overseas Development Administration (ODA) grew out of the old Colonial Office, and dependencies and ex-colonies are still favoured. In 1986, for example, the people of St Kitts-Nevis, 5 times richer than the citizens of Haiti, received 360 times as much aid per person. Political considerations also explain the £3 million given the same year to Belize, whose territory is claimed by Guatemala. They explain why Cuba receives no aid from Britain, Nicaragua a derisory £86,000 in 1986 and neighbouring Costa Rica as much as £11.5 million.

Need and the extent of poverty are not the criteria by which the ODA allocates aid to Latin America and the Caribbean. The desire to have token aid programmes in as many countries as possible and the wish to support US policy in the region are much more important.

The Sandinista government in Nicaragua has one of the best records of reaching and helping the poor in Latin America. Yet it is shown in Chapter 3 how the Thatcher government has consistently denied bilateral aid to that country and argued against aid supplied through the European Development Fund (EDF). In a memo about a delayed US$58 million loan from the IDB, an official wrote: 'We shall need to stick to our present line of claiming that our opposition is based on technical grounds'. In the margin a colleague commented, 'If we can find them!' The then Minister for Overseas Development, Timothy Raison, claimed that 'we have not sought to block any loans to Nicaragua', but in another memo an official wrote: 'I hope very much that in practice we will not be asked to oppose this one'.

Commercial factors as well as political ones have also had a distorting effect on overseas aid to the region. In 1982, the ODA provided £35 million to Mexico, one of the better-off Third World countries and an oil exporter, as part of the Aid-Trade Provision (ATP). The ATP, first introduced by Judith Hart and expanded under the Conservatives, enables aid to be used to help British companies win Third World contracts. Normally British aid to Mexico is only a few hundred thousand pounds a year. The £35 million ATP 'sweetener' helped Davy Loewy win a £200,000 contract to build a steel-plate mill at Sicartsa in Mexico. The British steel industry was in decline and in desperate need of contracts, but the world steel market was already over-supplied.

By 1986, 79 per cent of bilateral aid, including aid to Latin America, was tied to the purchase of British goods and services. This is in addition to a fall in real terms of 30 per cent in Britain's spending on overseas aid worldwide between 1979 and 1986. The British government likes to include in its aid output lending by the banks, private investment and voluntary giving to charities, such as Oxfam. By this yardstick, private and official flows to the Third World reached 1.34 per cent of British GNP in 1986, the ODA claims.

But in 1986, overseas aid to Latin America and the Caribbean was still negligible. Export credits saw a net repayment to Britain, and most of the flows consisted of 'involuntary' bank lending to Latin America, supplying credit for countries (mainly Mexico) to service their debts to the very same British banks.

Bailing out the banks

British banks lent heavily to Latin America in the 1970s, and the British government has insisted that borrowers service those debts. A huge cut in bank profits in 1987 should not disguise the fact that bankers have done very well out of their Latin American loans.

Lloyds, one of the 'big four' high-street banks, has a traditional involvement with the region. Lloyds itself has branches in Brazil, Paraguay and Guatemala, and its subsidiary, Bank of London and South America, in Argentina, Peru and Central America. Midland Bank acquired big Latin American debts when it took over the troubled Crocker Bank in the United States, which it has since sold. But most British banks fell over themselves in the 1970s to lend large sums to 'sovereign' Latin American customers. With the encouragement of Western governments they took on the role of recycling the petro-dollars deposited by the newly-rich oil states. At the time they believed the risk of sovereign governments going bust was small. But in the early 1980s the fall in commodity prices, the global recession and high interest rates – caused by the huge US budget deficit – combined to create the debt crisis.

At first, when borrowers could not afford to service their debts, the banks simply lent them more. But in 1982, Mexico effectively defaulted on its foreign debts, and US, British and other banks realised that their large outstanding loans were very risky indeed. By 1986, Latin America and the Caribbean owed US$388 billion on paper, and many countries could not pay the interest, let alone repay capital. The City of London was probably owed at least US$30 billion at this time, a relatively small part of the total but still a very large sum.

The banks tried to play down the importance of these loans, arguing that they represented 5 per cent or less of their total lending or assets. But these loans still represented between 69 per cent and 223 per cent of the funds of the banks' shareholders, the fundamental capital base of any bank. Banks operate by lending other people's money and rely on a steady income from those they lend to. If all the Latin American debtors had defaulted together, Lloyds and Midland could have gone bust and NatWest and Barclays would have made huge losses.

The international banks did not particularly want all their money back but they did want interest payments to be maintained, at almost any price. Western governments saw the International Monetary Fund (IMF) as the ideal police officer to make sure the debtors continued to pay. Nigel Lawson, Britain's Chancellor of the Exchequer and a member of the powerful IMF board, was determined to look after the interests of the UK banks. The IMF was prepared to lend to Latin American countries in difficulties, but only on very strict conditions. 'This means, first and foremost, allowing markets to work more freely', said Lawson in 1979. 'It means, in many cases, cutting back a bloated state sector. And it means keeping interest rates and the exchange rate at realistic levels', he added.

The IMF persuaded government after government to cut public spending, devalue the exchange rate and boost exports, to provide the cash to service the foreign debts. In return, the IMF and the banks agreed to 'roll over' repayment dates and to lend new money.

In 1984, Argentina was spending 29 per cent of its export income on servicing its foreign debt, Brazil 36 per cent and Mexico as much as 49 per cent. The result of prioritising debt repayments contributed to a massive fall in living standards and a net outflow of capital from the Caribbean and Latin America. As new loans dried up and Latin America kept paying its debts, every year from 1982 to 1986 saw a net outflow from the region to the West of around US$25 billion. The City of London effectively promoted the underdevelopment of the region. The income flow to the big four banks alone, for example, is estimated (by the Fabian Society in London) at between US$1.7 billion and US$2.4 billion between 1982 and 1985. In 1985, Lloyds and Midland, the most heavily exposed to Latin American lending, each obtained a quarter of their income from interest from that source. Barclays and NatWest still depended on the region for 10 per cent of their income from interest.

The big four will not say exactly how much profit they have made from Latin American business. But if that valuable income had suddenly been lost, it would have wiped out all Midland's pre-tax profits, three quarters of Lloyds' and a quarter of the profits of Barclays and NatWest.

For Latin American countries, the IMF solution caused severe deflation in their economies, but it allowed the international banks time to reduce their exposure to the increasingly non-performing loans of Latin America. They were able to pretend that the debts were still good in order to boost their profits.

In 1987, the British banks finally owned up and increased their bad-debt provisions to cover about 30 per cent of their Third World loans. In effect they admitted that £1 in every £3 lent to Latin America was never going to be repaid. The biggest bank, NatWest, was the first to write down its Third World debt portfolio. It was pushed into action by similar moves by Citicorp and Chase Manhattan in the United States and in the hope of gaining an advantage over its competitors. The other high-street banks followed suit and announced large cuts in their profits. But they remained as determined as ever to try to obtain every last penny or cent from their debtors in Latin America. The loans had been written down but not written off.

Nigel Lawson put forward a three-point plan to tackle the continuing debt crisis: converting aid loans into grants, extending repayment periods and reducing interest rates. But his plan was to apply only to Africa, not Latin America. Latin American nations 'are in a position to pull their own economies round and to reduce their debt burdens by their own actions', he claimed. 'It is clearly the joint responsibility of the debtor countries and the commercial banks to manage these debts', he said, denying the need for any government responsibility or intervention in the crisis. He added that he was opposed to taxpayers 'bailing out the banks'. But the big four alone are likely to receive at least £940 million in tax relief as a result of increasing their provisions against Third World debts and showing much smaller profits.

While the Chancellor was looking after the City, he was doing no favours for British exports to Latin America or for employment. The value of the region's imports fell by a third between 1980–2 and 1983–5 because of the debt squeeze. British exports to Latin America fell by US$1.5 billion between 1981 and 1985 and 200,000 jobs were lost because of the slump in Third World trade. High interest rates brought more cash into the banks, but partly at the cost of export orders for Britain. The debt crisis meant that in 1986 alone, US$22 billion more left Latin America and the Caribbean than went into the region. The City of London took its share; the British government offered the 'help' of the IMF.

Trade

It is not only as a financial centre but also as a world trading capital that London is involved with America south of the Río Grande. While British consumers have benefited from cheap Latin American exports, British companies have lost business in the continent. The region's external trade is overwhelmingly focused on North America, but Britain is a significant partner, especially for the Caribbean. Britain is part of the large European Community market, and London is an international centre for commodity trading.

The debt crisis has been accompanied by a serious recession in the world economy which has greatly depressed prices for the commodities on which so many Latin American countries still depend to pay off their debts. At the end of 1986, world commodity prices, measured against a basket of currencies, were a fifth lower than in 1980. The prices of tin and sugar were particularly badly hit, but the prices of nearly all commodities exported by Latin America were down.

Turning to all exports, including manufactured goods, the position has been equally bad. Since 1982, according to the 1987 IDB report, the volume of Latin American exports has risen by 19 per cent. But a fall of 21 per cent in the value of exports wiped out any gain in export earnings. Latin American traders have had to run to stand still. UNCTAD has calculated that the region lost an average of US$9 billion every year between 1981 and 1985. For the Western industrial countries, on the other hand, it has been estimated that more than half of the fall in the rate of increase in consumer prices between 1980 and 1984 was due to the fall in commodity prices. The Thatcher government's triumph over inflation has been half paid for by the Third World.

The biggest exporters of sugar during the Thatcher years were Cuba, the European Community, Brazil and Australia. The failure of the EEC to curb its overproduction helped depress the world market price of the crop. The EEC was a net sugar importer in the 1970s, but the expansion of sugar beet and its subsidised 'dumping' overseas wrecked any chance of an International Sugar Agreement. Britain and Britain's farmers bear some responsibility for this.

The Community did participate in an International Coffee Agreement intended to stabilise prices within an agreed price range. But in 1986, export quotas were suspended, and Britain was one of the consuming countries which resisted their reintroduction. Along with the United States and West Germany, it wanted to break the dominance of Brazil in the coffee market by forcing it to lose its traditional 30 per cent market share. The effect of the suspension of quotas was falling coffee prices for all Latin American exporters. A new agreement on quotas was finally reached in October 1987.

In 1986, the European Community – but not the United States – signed an International Cocoa Agreement which would adjust the price range in response to the market through the use of a buffer stock. Latin America exports only a fifth of the world's cocoa, but in the 1980s, Brazil became one of the largest exporters after four West African countries. But by 1987, Britain and other consumer nations were preventing the cocoa buffer stock from operating. The buffer-stock manager could not buy up surplus cocoa to bring about a rise in the cocoa price.

Britain was also a member of the ill-fated International Tin Agreement, which collapsed in 1985, with devastating results for Bolivia. Britain argued that the crash came about because tin prices were too high, but producers felt that the rich consumer nations underfinanced the Agreement's buffer stock. Dealers in tin on the London Metal Exchange made large losses from the collapse of the tin market, but in general, commodity dealers in London have continued to make considerable profits from their trade despite the fall in prices. In 1986, for example, Gill & Duffus made £39 million profit on commodity trading for the Dalgety parent company. Other leading companies with investments in Latin America have fared less well. High inflation, falling living standards and government spending cuts have all affected business in the region. The Anglo-Dutch conglomerate, Unilever, for example, complained in its 1985 annual report that 'trading conditions were not easy'. But the company was nevertheless able to make the best of the situation and in 1986 purchased a majority stake in Anderson Clayton, which markets margarine in Brazil and Mexico. In 1987, it could report that results from its food and detergent business in Latin America were much improved.

British American Tobacco (BAT), the world's largest tobacco corporation, is another UK company deeply involved in Latin America. It has majority stakes in, or owns outright, subsidiary companies in 15 Caribbean and Latin American nations. It owns, for instance, *Cigarros Souza Cruz* in Brazil, *Chiletabacos*, and *Cigarros Bigott* in Venezuela, as well as a majority stake in *Tabacalera Nicaragüense*. In the early 1980s, the board found it difficult to sell cigarettes to Latin Americans who were becoming poorer each year. Chairman Patrick Sheehy even made representations to the British government about IMF austerity, but to little effect. By 1986 Latin America was providing BAT with £148 million in pre-tax profits or 10 per cent of its worldwide income.

'The merits of the present world economic system'

Back in 1980, Willy Brandt, the former West German Chancellor, had argued for greater co-operation between North and South. He asserted that helping the world's poor nations would also mean expanding markets for the rich countries and would avert an impending recession. The Brandt Report was disregarded by Britain and other Western countries in their determination to damp down inflation. Mrs Thatcher was deeply opposed to the philosophy behind the report and rejected its ideas out of hand: 'The government believes strongly in the merits of the present world economic system, with its reliance on open markets', said the Foreign Office in July 1980; 'the system has regularly and flexibly adapted to changing conditions.'

In the ensuing years, the world plunged into recession: trade slumped, unemployment rocketed and living standards fell. Britain was able to export its inflation to the Third World, where the poor bore the brunt of the monetarist dogma. By the mid-1980s, Britain was pulling out of recession while Latin America remained deep in slump. The Thatcher government continues to refuse any consideration of international governmental action to assist Latin America's recovery. Its insistence that private enterprise and the market can solve the region's problems is essentially ideological. Mrs Thatcher is contributing to a system which condemns millions of Latin American poor to continued, but preventable, misery.

3. Under attack: Central America and the Caribbean

Central America and the Caribbean are not of great importance to Britain. In economic terms the region represents a very low percentage of British global levels of investment, trade and aid, and in political terms it has a low priority compared to Britain's major areas of foreign policy concern in the Middle East, South Africa and the NATO Alliance. There are, of course, strong historical links, particularly with the Commonwealth Caribbean, and a military commitment of 1,800 British troops in the former British colony of Belize. But for the Thatcher government, the whole region is seen as the proper concern of the US, and Britain's role is to give crucial international support for its policies.

Given Mrs Thatcher's 'special relationship' with President Reagan and the degree of ideological overlap between them, it is hardly surprising that Mrs Thatcher should faithfully mirror the Reagan vision of Central America. If she is prepared to accept the political cost of allowing Britain to be used as a base for the F1-11s to bomb Libya, it is entirely predictable that she would support Reagan's policies in an area where the political cost for Britain is much less. On very few occasions Whitehall has expressed some reservations about US actions – when President Reagan tried to resume arms sales to Guatemala in 1982, when British vessels were threatened after the mining of Nicaraguan ports at Washington's instigation in 1984, and when Britain was not 'properly consulted' over the invasion of Grenada in 1983. For the most part, however, British government policy stands condemned for its failure to develop a line or an analysis independent of the Reagan administration. Nowhere is this uncritical support more evident than in the British government's failure – despite its claim to support a political solution to the problems of the region – to make a strong and unequivocal condemnation of the terrorism of the contras or the US role in guaranteeing their political survival.

The extent to which ideology has become a major factor in foreign policy is clearly visible in British policy towards the region. The British government's hostility to the progressive governments which came to power in Grenada and Nicaragua in 1979 contrasts dramatically to its support for the Duarte government in El Salvador and the Cerezo government in Guatemala. The Nicaraguan government is reviled for its lack of pluralism and suspension of civil liberties, while the Salvadorean government is

26

praised for its efforts to restore democracy. Observers are not sent to the Nicaraguan election, but they are sent to the Salvadorean. Yet, no centre/left candidate could stand in the Salvadorean election for fear of assassination, while seven parties from conservatives to the far-left stood in the Nicaraguan elections. In the 'low-intensity democracies' of El Salvador and Guatemala, hundreds of people are still murdered or 'disappeared' by the security forces, who remain untried and laws unto themselves. In Nicaragua the death penalty has been abolished, political opponents are not disappeared or tortured, and members of the security forces who commit abuses are tried and jailed. Cerezo's Guatemala receives diplomatic recognition; Duarte's El Salvador is rewarded with UK training for a military cadet; Sandinista Nicaragua is punished for daring to challenge Britain's cold war ally.

El Salvador

The Thatcher government has presented its policies towards El Salvador in terms of concern for the rule of law and democracy, respect for human rights and a preference for political solutions to the country's civil war. In practice, it has given crucial support to the Reagan administration's intervention in that country, which, as we shall see, has worked against the achievement of all these objectives.

British concern with human rights violations in El Salvador dates back to the late 1970s. In 1978, Dr David Owen, then the Labour government's Foreign Secretary, announced that there would be no more arms sales to El Salvador until there were changes in the human rights situation. He exempted an £850,000 shipment of armoured cars already in the pipeline, but was subsequently forced to cancel it after a major public campaign.

At the end of 1978 an all-party British Parliamentary Delegation (Lord Chitnis, Peter Bottomley and Dennis Canavan) visited El Salvador to assess for themselves the human rights situation. Their conclusion presaged the violent conflict that was shortly to unfold:

> In our opinion, the path which the present government of El Salvador is following and its gross violations of human rights . . . have led to a growing polarisation and can only end in violent tragedy reminiscent of the masscres of 1932. If this tragedy is to be averted there must be a radical change of direction in government policies and the restoration of democratic freedoms. In an entrenched military dictatorship such as El Salvador, this is unlikely to happen overnight. In order for it to happen at all, the immediate first steps should include:
>
> 1. A general amnesty for all political prisoners, including particularly those who have 'disappeared'.
> 2. The repeal of the Law of Public Order.
> 3. Recognition under the law of peasant unions and the attendant right to organise freely.

4. The initiation of a wide-ranging dialogue with political parties, trades union, peasant organisations and the Church to discuss the acute and pressing problems confronting Salvadorean society.
5. Effective international supervision of the next series of elections in El Salvador to safeguard the democratic process.

These measures were not, however, to be implemented. In October 1979, less than a year after the parliamentarians' visit, President Romero was overthrown in a coup. Despite initial indications that progressive officers were involved in the coup and that reforming political parties would benefit, it soon became clear that the right wing of the army was very much in control. Indeed, the months following the coup saw a terrible escalation in human rights abuses. The measures which the parliamentarians had considered prerequisites for the restoration of democratic freedoms were not on the agenda.

Instead, the United States stepped in with its own priorities for the country. Foremost among these was a counter-insurgency drive to wipe out the guerrilla forces operating in the country and to suppress the popular movement which lay behind the guerrillas' growing strength. As 200,000 people took to the streets of San Salvador in March 1980 to protest against the assassination of Archbishop Romero, US analysts recognised the need for rapid action if El Salvador was not to follow Nicaragua along the path of revolution. The first steps were taken under the Carter administration; when President Reagan came into office in January 1981, US involvement escalated dramatically.

The US-sponsored counter-insurgency programme was typical of many it had launched in the Third World since techniques were tested in Vietnam in the 1960s. It involved a combination of repression, even terror, and more sophisticated methods of winning popular support and international legitimacy for the US-backed government.

The Reagan-Duarte alliance
The US was fortunate in El Salvador to have the collaboration of a major Christian Democrat politician, José Napoleón Duarte. Duarte had been a respected and popular figure in the country; a former mayor of San Salvador, he was deprived of the presidency in 1972 by a fraud. He was also an ambitious man, and when his party split over support for the junta, which had theoretically been running the country until March 1980, Duarte opted to become its new head. His Christian Democrat predecessor on the junta, Hector Dada, resigned because, he declared, 'we have not been able to stop the repression, and those committing acts of repression . . . go unpunished; the promised dialogue with the popular organisations fails to materialize; the chances for producing reforms with the support of the people are receding beyond reach'.

Duarte went on to become a central figure in US strategy towards the country. His importance lay in his ability to legitimate this strategy both internationally and to the US public and Congress. This importance grew over the years, despite his defeat in the 1982 elections and a period out of office. As a civilian and head of a democratic party with a record of commitment to reform, he helped sustain the view that the Salvadorean government and US policies were genuinely concerned with the plight of the poor. Human rights abuses were blamed on the extreme right-wing death squads, over which, it was claimed, the government had no control. The Thatcher government has frequently echoed this view in public and in private.

In reality, the violation of human rights has been a corollary of the policies pursued by the Salvadorean and US governments. These have given priority to the repression of the opposition movement. As such, virtually limitless power has been placed in the hands of the Salvadorean army, greatly strengthened by US military aid and training. It is the Salvadorean army which has carried out the vast majority of the killings which since 1980 have taken over 55,000 lives. As the Liberal peer, Lord Chitnis, has written: 'to put the emphasis on the death squads is to disregard the fact that the government's conduct of the civil war is the major cause of violent death in El Salvador today'.

No high-ranking member of the army or security forces has yet been brought to justice for what have often been barbarous murders, among them that of four US nuns. Justice and the rule of law are essentially incompatible with a US military strategy which, as in Vietnam, justifies any action by armies intent on defeating 'communism'. In this way, the Salvadorean army has become the real power centre in El Salvador, able to act with virtual impunity. It has been so throughout the period of Duarte's government, though Duarte himself has helped, through his presence in the government, to conceal this. Far from strengthening democracy in El Salvador, US policies have enhanced the power of the institution most dangerous to it.

The US government of El Salvador

The US government has become the major policy maker in the country, not the Salvadorean government. It not only finances the war, it also gives considerable economic aid and has prevented the economic collapse which would otherwise undoubtedly have taken place. Altogether it has provided some US$3.3 billion in military and economic aid between 1981 and 1987. El Salvador is the third largest recipient of US military aid, after Israel and Egypt.

The priority given by the US and its Salvadorean allies to a military solution to the war has meant that the highly publicised government reform programme was mostly concerned with the counter-insurgency strategy rather than with the real needs of the poor majority. For instance, the third phase of the land reform, hastily announced in 1980, was even drawn up by the same man, Roy Prosterman, who had carried out the 'land to the tiller' programme in Vietnam. It showed little understanding of the particular problems of rural El Salvador, such as the infertility of much of the land farmed by small tenant farmers for whom title to the land was a necessary, but hardly sufficient, step towards making a living from it. Its main objective was political: to win the backing of a section of the small-farming population through giving them a plot of land and thus a 'stake in the system'. The first phase of the reform which turned mostly cattle ranching land over to its workers to form co-operatives has also run into serious problems as a result of hasty preparation, poor agricultural land and the lack of financing.

Given the real problem of the relationship of population to resources in El Salvador, only a thorough land reform which tackles the general problem of land ownership and use could contribute to a solution. In particular, it would have to deal with the concentration of land in the hand of a few, very wealthy, powerful families, known as the oligarchy. But the oligarchy has been allowed essentially to veto such a possibility. Those parts of the reform which might have affected its land have never been implemented.

Most independent observers who have investigated the agrarian reform have drawn attention to its failure to solve the land problem which lies behind El Salvador's civil war. But, politically, the mere fact of the reform's existence on paper has allowed the US to argue that its policies towards the country are not purely military. The Thatcher government has made frequent use of this argument in order to justify its own support for US policies in El Salvador.

The British connection

The British government support on El Salvador has been extremely important to the US, which otherwise would have faced embarrassing international isolation. In 1982, the US was struggling to maintain credibility for its policies in the face of the mounting toll of violent deaths in the country and widespread condemnation of the role of the army and security forces in perpetrating them. An election was called for a Constituent Assembly to give legitimacy to the political process and enable the government to pursue the war without the degree of international opprobrium it had hitherto encountered. The expectation was that Duarte and the Christian Democrats would head the poll.

The US sent out 60 invitations to carefully selected governments to send observers; only Costa Rica, Uruguay, Egypt, Colombia and Britain agreed to do so. A West German spokesman summed up the view of many European governments when he said: 'such elections are themselves a matter of dispute among groups within El Salvador. By sending observers, we would be appearing to take a position.' In March 1982, the European parliament said that elections in El Salvador could not be regarded as free.

The country was in the throes of a murderous civil war, in which right-wing death squads kidnapped, tortured and killed suspected guerrilla sympathisers, and the army and security forces (whose members frequently dressed as civilians to form the death squads at night) carried out brutal massacres of peasants during their regular sweeps in search of guerrillas. There was no respect for civil liberties, no freedom of the press and no independent judiciary. In such circumstances, the progressive opposition forces, which in desperation had joined forces with the FMLN guerrillas to become their political wing (the FDR) in 1980, could not have risked participating. The elections were therefore restricted to the right and centre-right.

Nevertheless, Britain sent its two observers, Sir John Galsworthy and Professor Derek Bowett. It did so at the same time as it declared its desire for a peaceful solution to the civil war, knowing that the US had ruled out any negotiations with the guerrillas and that the elections would strengthen its ability to pursue a military solution to the civil war.

Lord Chitnis subsequently wrote a stinging indictment of the way the British observers undertook their task (see box). He stated his own conclusions in his 1982 report for the Parliamentary Human Rights Group: 'It is clear to me that the result of this strange, foreign-inspired election cannot be said to represent what in normal circumstances would be a free and unfettered choice of the people of El Salvador about their future.' Subsequent evidence produced by researchers from the Central American University in San Salvador concluded that the vote total had been inflated by fraudulent means by at least 450,000 votes. 'We didn't denounce the fraud', Hugo Barrera of the extreme right-wing ARENA party later told a Canadian journalist, 'because we didn't want to spoil the good result and image of the election.'

The Christian Democrats did not win the elections; the extreme right took control of the Constituent Assembly. Under pressure from the US, a 'moderate' unknown banker, Alvaro Magana, was nominated provisional President rather than Roberto D'Aubuisson, candidate of the extreme right. But the two years leading up to the presidential elections of 1984 proved very bad for the US. The guerrillas gained in strength and effectiveness. The repression against all those suspected of sympathy with them continued, bringing wide international condemnation of the government and creating difficulties for the Reagan administration in raising money for the war from Congress. In November 1983, only 12 countries voted (in addition to the US and the Salvadorean governments) against a UN resolution expressing 'deep concern' at the violation of human rights. All the countries of Scandinavia and the EEC voted in favour of the resolution, except Britain and West Germany, who abstained.

Lord Chitnis describes the political developments of these years as 'more the result of bargaining between the Reagan administration and the Salvadorean armed forces than any discernible democratic processes'. Considerable efforts were made to pave the way for Duarte's victory in the 1984 elections. He travelled to Europe in 1983 and press reports noted that 'Mrs Thatcher has ordered her Foreign Office staff to give [him] a special welcome.'

Once again the British government sent observers, Sir James Swaffield and Dr David Browning, to both rounds of the 1984 elections. The US had poured money into Duarte's campaign: almost US$1 million had been channelled through the CIA, according to the *New York Times*, and the US had computerised the electoral register which, in the event, caused considerable administrative chaos, particularly in the first round.

The reports of the observers can be criticised on many points, but they did make more of an effort to escape the security vigilance which shadowed their predecessors, and they talked to a wider body of opinion. In their report they were forced to admit that the FDR–FMLN would not have been able to participate freely and securely in the election campaign, but they did not face up to the implications of this: that the radical alternative was not placed before the electorate, making the election, in the words of Lord Chitnis in the 1984 report to the Parliamentary Human Rights Group, 'a contest of vague promises and inferences about the future between two candidates (Duarte and Roberto D'Aubuisson of ARENA), each of whom bears a heavy responsibility for the situation in which El Salvador finds itself today'.

Unlike the British government observers, Lord Chitnis, who went as an independent observer to the second round, drew attention to the context in which the elections took place. His general conclusion was:

An election was held within a very limited range of the political spectrum; choices were given but very few; an electoral process took place which in terms of its administration was not too bad – indeed, given the over-sophisticated system wished on the country by its wealthy friends, people coped remarkably well in the second round.

But he points out:

> Unless President Duarte prefers to show himself, as he promised to be, a President of all Salvadoreans, capable of controlling those who would usurp his authority and directly or indirectly cause even more deaths in that tragic land, then the election will be seen to have been an irrelevant, divisive and expensive exercise. El Salvador is full of people who care nothing about the PDC, ARENA, indelible ink and Wang computers, but about life, peace, social justice and freedom. Only if their voice is heard will anything that has happened in El Salvador during the first half of 1984 be worthwhile.

Elections, but no democracy

Lord Chitnis has highlighted the real issue, which is not the mere fact that an election took place in 1984, but whether that election could contribute to a solution to those problems which plunged the country into civil war. Unfortunately, many (among them the British government) were content merely to see an election take place and assume that there had been a transfer of power.

Nothing in fact changed in 1984; the army was as much at the centre of power as ever and able to veto any attempt at a negotiated solution to the war and any reforms which might affect the richest section of society. Duarte was able to deliver on none of his promises to bring peace and introduce reforms. Under great pressure from the US (who after all was its paymaster) there was some reduction in human rights violations by the army in order to appease US congressional and international opinion. But nobody was brought to justice for past crimes, repression still continued, albeit more selectively, and there was no guarantee that it would not escalate once again if the popular movement recovered from the terror used against it in the past.

Duarte did succeed in bringing credibility to US policies in El Salvador. His post-election visit to Washington proved enormously successful in winning support from Congress for continued military and economic aid to his government. The guerrilla forces came under great pressure as the war was taken to the air, and bombardment of guerrilla-held areas (which mostly affected their civilian supporters and broke all international conventions) and the use of special lasers to detect movements of troops at night from the air forced them to abandon any large-scale operations.

The confidence that Duarte inspired, now that El Salvador had a properly elected President, was reflected in the British government's increased support. Confidential documents, obtained by the *New Statesman*, revealed that on 25 October 1984, the government had instructed its delegation to the World Bank to stop 'opposing or abstaining on all proposals' and instead support all 'developmentally-sound projects' in El Salvador. There was 'no need to publicise [this] change' in policy, according to the documents. The instructions were signed by James Watt, who formely ran the El Salvador desk at the Foreign Office, and he set out the official 'line' if the change in policy was discovered: 'if challenged we should be ready to defend it, as we defend our resumption of aid to El Salvador'.

Almost at the same time, in November 1984, a decision was taken to reintroduce a small aid programme to El Salvador, consisting of a grant of £100,000 for the purchase of civilian supplies and equipment and a plan for scholarships for postgraduate studies in Great Britain. The government also offered military training at staff colleges in Britain to 'one or two suitably qualified Salvadorean military officers'. After considerable public protest, only one young cadet was offered training; he began a course at Sandhurst in January 1987.

This policy was justified by the claim that it would expose the cadet to the 'high professional standards and democratic values which prevail in Western Europe, from where most of the students come'. Even if this were the case (and it should be remembered that Sandhurst also trained Idi Amin and General Zia ul Haq of Pakistan), the potential good for one cadet is hardly likely to influence an army which has such a bloody record as that of El Salvador. More important is the symbolic nature of the gesture of support for the Salvadorean government and its policies, despite its human rights record. The British government had itself finally acknowleged this record when in December 1985 it voted with 99 other countries at the UN to condemn El Salvador's human rights violations.

Conclusion

In its policy statement of January 1987, the Foreign Office stated that its objectives in El Salvador (and Central America as a whole) were 'to support friendly Governments in consolidating democratic institutions and the rule of law, to encourage economic and social development, and to end insurgency and terrorism'. The statement goes on to express support for the Duarte government, which, it claims, 'is widely recognised to be trying to improve the human rights situation. [Duarte's] government is facing a destructive war by an insurgent group which has declined to participate in democratic elections, and to put its support to the test through the ballot box'.

Even the government's own election observers had had to admit that it would have been very risky for the opposition parties to participate in the elections. Duarte's government has in fact done very little to improve the human rights record of its country. It has brought almost nobody to trial for murder or torture. The decline in repression in recent years has been mostly due to pressure from the US when congressional approval for military aid made it necessary to 'clean up' the image of the Salvadorean army; it was unlikely anyway that the death toll would remain at the extreme levels of the first years of the war. Even so, according to the human rights office of the Catholic Archdiocese, 1,725 civilians lost their lives in army counter-insurgency operations and 42 civilians were killed by right-wing death squads, and an estimated 300 civilians died in airforce bombing raids from January to October 1986.

1987 saw a further deterioration in the human rights situation and in the stability of the Duarte government. Duarte's failure to deliver on any of his promises, particularly to bring peace and improve living standards, greatly undermined the support he had won in the 1984 elections. Strikes and the first demonstrations for many years expressed the desperation of people who were prepared to risk their lives on the streets to protest against the misery of their situation. With unemployment estimated at 50 per cent of the population and a third of the workforce living below the minimum wage, people were living in dire conditions, exacerbated by the earthquake of October 1986.

The British government's faith in Duarte has not been based on any considered analysis of the balance of forces in the country. This would have told them that Duarte may have won an election in 1984, but he did not win power. He achieved his lifelong ambition of the presidency, but it was a pyrrhic victory. He cannot make any moves without the backing of the army. The army and the US are determined to defeat the guerrilla forces militarily and will prolong the war with that end in view. Duarte has merely facilitated this policy by giving civilian credibility to what is, in many senses, a military government. Although the peace initiatives of President Arias of Costa Rica have put peace on the agenda in El Salvador, as elsewhere in the region, Duarte has made it very clear that it is peace on the terms laid down by the army, i.e. that the guerrilla forces must first lay down their arms.

The British government's policies are based on a political decision to back the US administration in a country of little interest to the UK. But even within its own terms the policy is short-sighted. There will be no lasting stability in El Salvador until the root causes of the civil war are dealt with. Peace in El Salvador depends on the creation of a new and just social order. This will not be achieved while the army and the privileged classes retain political power.

Nicaragua *

The following recommendations on Nicaragua were proposed by the House of Commons Foreign Affairs Committee in 1982:

> With regard to Nicaragua, we feel that the single factor most likely to determine future developments there will be the attitude of the United States. Whether or

* The section on Nicaragua draws heavily on a booklet entitled *The British Connection*, published by the Nicaragua Solidarity Campaign in 1987.

not there is justification for the present Nicaraguan fear of United States direct or indirect aggression, the United Kingdom should use its influence with both parties to reduce present US Nicaraguan mutual misunderstandings . . . With regard to bilateral relations between the United Kingdom and Nicaragua we recommend that efforts be made to increase the present very low level of political, economic and cultural contacts between the two nations . . . We recommend that Britain should consider economic aid to Nicaragua; the HMG should work to ensure appropriate economic and financial help to Nicaragua from multilateral institutions; that Britain should consider how best to increase our economic assistance, our trade and our cultural exchanges with Nicaragua; and that the main aim of British policy should be to support the aspirations of those Nicaraguans who desire a truly pluralist society and mixed economy.

The Committee was made up of both Conservative and Labour Party MPs; a number of the Conservatives were on the right of the party and viewed the world very much through the lens of the Cold War. But while they acknowledged the importance of the Atlantic Alliance, they were also Europeans. And as Europeans they clearly did not swallow whole the Reaganite view of the origins of conflict in the Caribbean basin. They recognised that there were other perspectives than East-West ones on that conflict, and that many of Britain's allies and partners in Europe and Latin America gave as much or more weight to the internal causes of the conflict than to any alleged external interference. It is perhaps with this in mind that they emphasise the need for a specifically *British* policy towards the nations of Central America, based on 'our own ability to make an informed appreciation of the national aspirations and developments within each'.

The report expresses sympathy with the view of a number of witnesses to the Committee that Britain and its EEC partners should encourage dialogue with the United States and with concerned Latin American countries about alternative ways of approaching the problems of Central America. In the extract quoted above, for instance, Britain is seen as a mediator between the United States and Nicaragua.

In other words, despite the concern shared by the Conservative members of the Committee with the United States' 'legitimate security interests' in the Caribbean basin, they did not believe that Britain should align itself uncritically with the US administration's interpretation of where these were threatened. The spirit of the report is for an independent British policy on the region in general and Nicaragua in particular; it has been virtually completely ignored.

Policy based on ideology

Prime Minister Thatcher's policies towards Nicaragua have not been based on the kind of sober assessment seen in the Committee report. They are rooted in the ideology of the Cold War. Nicaragua's widely recognised efforts to meet the needs of the majority of its population through better health care, education, land distribution and community participation have had little or no influence on policy makers in this country. It is the perception of the country's role in the East-West divide, mostly fed to it by the Reagan administration, which has determined British policy.

Mrs Thatcher herself of course shares much of the world view of President Reagan. Her own comments on Nicaragua (very rare though they are) echo his own, such as her statement in the House of Commons on 14 February 1985:

> Vice President Ramirez called on me on 8 February at his own request. I expressed my concern about the substantial build up of arms, troops and foreign military advisers in Nicaragua and Nicaraguan support for attempts to destabilise democratic Governments elsewhere in Central America. I made clear that the Government's future relations with Nicaragua would be determined by progress towards establishing genuine democracy there, scaling down of armaments and the cessation of support for subversion.

Each one of Mrs Thatcher's concerns is based on arguments frequently used by the Reagan adminstration to justify its highly publicised efforts to overthrow the elected government of Nicaragua. Each one is also highly questionable. The undoubted increase in the Sandinista army's strength and its acquisition of new weapons are directly related to the escalation of US support for the contras, who would undoubtedly collapse without US military and economic aid. The Nicaraguans also have the very genuine fear that US marines could eventually invade – a fear based on the historical fact that they have done so on five occasions in Nicaragua, and throughout the region on frequent occasions, in the course of the 20th century. Moreover, there is overwhelming evidence that the Nicaraguan arms build-up is essentially defensive and not offensive in nature. They have no modern attack aircraft, whereas Honduras – the country they would be most likely to be accused of invading – has the largest and strongest airforce in the region. The tanks they possess are unsuitable for offensive operations due to Central America's terrain, and cannot seriously be considered a threat when neither Honduras nor El Salvador has acquired anti-tank weapons. Lieutenant-Colonel Buchanan, a former US marine, testified to US Congress that the Nicaraguan army had neither the ground forces, the tanks nor the back-up aircraft to make an invasion feasible. He added that 'my assessment of Nicaraguan military power leads me to believe that the capabilities of the Sandinistas have been deliberately exaggerated by the Reagan administration'.

The allegation that Nicaragua exports subversion is equally unfounded. As *The British Connection* argued:

> The American military in El Salvador has the world's most sophisticated spy-satellite and radar equipment, covering the whole of Central America, and yet it has never produced any evidence of Nicaragua smuggling or exporting arms. American arms supplies to the contra have been well publicised following the shooting down of a CIA plane ferrying supplies to contras inside Nicaragua in

October 1986, yet no Nicaraguan has ever been captured smuggling arms in Honduras, Costa Rica, or El Salvador . . . The Salvadorean guerrillas have been fighting an army of 45,000 army troops for seven years it is inconceivable that Nicaragua could have supplied arms for that long and not have been spotted by the US.

The criticism that Nicaragua is not democratic is largely based on political prejudice. In 1984, Nicaragua held elections under the glare of the world's media and a vast array of international observers. The British government was the only European government not to send official observers. But independent British observers from all political parties returned convinced that the elections were fair. Conservative MP David Ashby said 'I was able to observe unhindered the electoral process, and could detect no suspicion of malpractice. The elections were properly carried out', while Lord Chitnis stated that 'the election in Nicaragua was superior in every major respect to the election in El Salvador'. The seven parties contesting the elections ranged from the far left to liberals and conservatives, and since the elections they have participated in the National Assembly and in January 1987 agreed a new Constitution.

The fact that there were no official British observers at the Nicaraguan election has not prevented the government from consistently questioning their fairness and hence the legitimacy of the Sandinista government. For example, the June 1987 Foreign Office policy statement on Nicaragua wrote on the elections: 'we concluded from our observation of the election campaign in 1984 that the non-Sandinista parties did not enjoy the same rights or ability to campaign as the Sandinistas'. Apart from the fact that those British politicians who attended and monitored the elections did not agree with this, it is worth noting that the official British observers which were sent to the Salvadorean elections in 1984, concluded that the opposition FDR/FMLN could not safely participate in the elections in that country, yet the British government nevertheless considered those elections as valid and fair.

Irrespective of the merits of the arguments, Mrs Thatcher is clearly prepared slavishly to repeat Reagan's objections to the Sandinistas. There are many in the Conservative Party and in the Foreign Office who are critical of the Sandinistas but who nevertheless do not share – and even fear the consequences of – a policy based on such an uncritical acceptance of Reagan's personal crusade against Nicaragua. Some worry that the contras' inability to overthrow the Sandinistas might lead to a direct US intervention and hence destabilise NATO, while others tend to consider the broader European position which, apart from West Germany after the election of Chancellor Kohl, has distinguished itself clearly from that of the Reagan administration (see box). But Mrs Thatcher's 'special relationship' and ideological sympathy with Reagan seem to have dominated British policy, as only on very rare occasions has the British government not followed the US line.

Britain, Europe and Nicaragua

In general, European governments have been more supportive of the Sandinista government than Britain. This is especially true of economic aid, as an estimated 40 per cent of all European aid to Central America goes to Nicaragua. In contrast, from 1979–86 only 1.4 per cent of bilateral British aid to Central America went to Nicaragua. While British aid to Nicaragua totalled US$1.4 million from 1979–85, Dutch aid came to US$115 million over the same period, Swedish aid US$75 million, Italian aid US$35 million, and French aid US$20 million. Even Finland and the conservative government of Switzerland have given many times more aid to Nicaragua than has Britain.

The Reagan administration has found it difficult to persuade the rest of Europe to adopt an anti-Sandinista stance. At a September 1984 meeting of EEC foreign ministers at San José, Costa Rica, each of the delegates received a letter from US Secretary of State, George Shultz, urging that the meeting should 'not lead to increased economic aid or any political support for Nicaragua'. EEC unity remained firm, and Nicaragua was included as a full partner in the regional aid package. The US-supported attempt by the contras' political wing, the United Nicaraguan Opposition (UNO), to bring the EEC round to a pro-contra position was frustrated when the contras were refused access to the European Parliament in May 1986. Britain has nevertheless tried at times to influence the EEC into adopting more anti-Sandinista positions. For example, at a crucial meeting of the GATT in May 1985 in Geneva to discuss the US trade embargo of Nicaragua, Britain was reported to have insisted before the debate to its European partners that it would not agree to any EEC statement implying criticism of the US.

Britain has also lobbied at the UN in favour of US positions against Nicaragua. When Nicaragua took the World Court ruling on the illegality of US actions to the UN General Assembly, Britain abstained – a surprising move when Britain accepts the compulsory jurisdiction of the World Court. The British representative, Sir John Thomson, also accused Nicaragua of using the World Court judgment for 'narrow political ends'. As *The Times* reported, 'in stark contrast to the majority view that the Sandinista government is an innocent victim of Washington's bullying, Sir John said that the crisis besetting Nicaragua was largely of its own making'.

On some issues, West Germany has joined Britain in its dissent. During the EEC-Central America meetings in 1985, West Germany sought to exclude Nicaragua by insisting that funds earmarked for development projects be linked to the proviso that governments must safeguard human rights and democratic liberties. Nevertheless, in May 1987 President Arias of Costa Rica did manage to gain backing from West German Foreign Minister Hans-Dietrich Genscher for his Peace Plan for Central America. Although the Peace Plan also received strong support from the EEC Commission, Spain and Portugal, the British government was studiously cautious when Arias came to London. A statement from Downing Street made it clear that 'it was not for the British government to endorse his proposals as such'.

Aid as politics

Perhaps the best evidence for the extent to which Britain has followed the US line is the way bilateral or multilateral aid to Nicaragua has been cut or blocked by the Thatcher government. Britain and the USA are the only major aid donors who gave more aid in the last seven years of the Somoza dictatorship than they have given in the first seven years of the revolution. This is despite the fact that development agencies in Britain have been unanimous in their assertion that Nicaragua offers the most conducive environment for carrying out development work in the whole of the Central American region. Oxfam went so far as to publish a book highlighting this fact, entitled *The Threat of a Good Example*. Indeed, if any country fulfils the government's own stated priorities for giving aid ('a greater focus of resources . . . where local policies seem likely to be supportive of aid efforts'), it is Nicaragua.

The record on British aid to Nicaragua compared to that of other European countries is very poor (see box page). As significant as the low level of aid to Nicaragua, is the amount of aid given to US allies in the Central American region which already receive substantial amounts of aid. In 1985, Honduras received £3.6 million from the UK government (US$231 million from the USA), Costa Rica received £12.5 million (US$198 million from the USA), while Nicaragua received £116,000 from the UK and, of course, nothing from the US government. In *The Threat of a Good Example*, Oxfam recommends that the British government should increase its bilateral aid to Nicaragua to a comparable level with Honduras and assess aid to Nicaragua solely on development criteria.

Britain also sends aid to Nicaragua through the multilateral agencies of which it is a member. But it has done its best to oppose such aid in these agencies. It has expressed strong political opposition to increased aid to Nicaragua within the EEC and in 1982 tried, unsuccessfully, to block an aid project. In one notorious incident, documents leaked from the Overseas Development Administration (ODA) in 1985 showed very clearly how the British government has tried to block loans to Nicaragua in the World Bank and Inter American Development Bank. (see page 20)

Terrorism and peace

The British government has repeatedly confirmed its opposition to terrorism, from whatever source. It has also repeatedly expressed its support for a peaceful solution to the conflict in Central America. In its 1987 statement on Nicaragua, the Foreign Office wrote: 'we have made it clear that we advocate a political solution to the problems of Central America on the basis of the Contadora objectives rather than a military solution. We do not believe the problems of the area can be resolved by armed force'. But the British government has never made a strong and forthright statement condemning the terrorism of the contras or the US government's role in funding them.

The silence becomes deafening when regular reports by Amnesty International, Americas Watch and other human rights organisations have documented contra atrocities including murder, torture, multilation, rape, arson and kidnapping. Perhaps as many as 20,000 Nicaraguans have died as a result of contra activities. Terror is clearly an instrument of contra policy. As Edgar Chamorro, a former contra official, has stated:

> It is cynical to think that the contra respect human rights. During my four years as a contra director, it was premeditated practice to terrorise civilian non-combatants to prevent their cooperation with the government . . . no serious effort has been made to stop them because terror is the most effective weapon of the contra.

Nevertheless, Arturo Cruz, formerly one of the three leaders of the contra political arm, has spoken on at least two occasions at private conferences in London in 1985 and 1986. Moreover, in June 1986 the World Court at The Hague ruled that the US was guilty on eight counts of breaching international law in its covert and contra war against Nicaragua. Out of a total of 15 judges, only the British and Japanese representatives backed the US. Since the ruling, Britain has made no effort to press the Reagan administration to respect the court's decision.

While paying lip service to the need for a non-military solution to the conflict, the Thatcher government has been repeatedly accused of supplying arms and training to the contras. The main evidence for the allegations surfaced during the Iran-contra enquiry, where British companies and individuals emerged as key figures in Lieutenant-Colonel Oliver North's clandestine arms network.

The Iran-contra hearings highlighted two main areas of British involvement: the attempt to supply surface-to-air missiles, and the training and sabotage operations of security firms run by a network of former SAS officers. In a third, so far unconnected, case, a British ship was intercepted by French authorities at the start of an gun-running trip to Costa Rica.

In all three cases there is no hard evidence of open British military and logistical support to the contras. Many suspect that government involvement goes deeper, at least to the point of knowing about the operations prior to their taking place. In each case British law was probably broken, but at the time of writing no charges have been brought (see box).

Britain, Guatemala and Belize

Since 1979, the Thatcher government has spent around £25 million a year on keeping up to 1,800 British troops stationed in a small ex-colony of 150,000 inhabitants. That country, Belize, is in fact a full member of the United Nations and is soon to be accepted as a member of the Organisation of

Blowpipe diplomacy

The blowpipe missile is a simple and effective surface-to-air missile, long coveted by Lieutenant-Colonel North and the contra leadership as the ideal counter to the Sandinistas' extremely effective helicopter fleet. It is manufactured by Short Bros of Belfast, a government-owned company.

As revealed in the Tower Commission report into the Iran-contra affair, North, in a memo to the then National Security Adviser Robert MacFarlane, said: 'we are trying to find a way to get 10 Blowpipe launchers and 20 missiles . . . Short Bros, the manufacturer of the Blowpipe, is willing to arrange the deal, conduct the training and even send UK "tech reps"'. North told MacFarlane he had arranged payment of 10 per cent of Short Bros' fee. The *Los Angeles Times* reported that the British government had given 'preliminary approval' for the deal. The approval was needed for export licenses, and relied on the use of bogus 'end user certificates' obtained either from the CIA or a 'South American country', probably Chile.

The government denies ever even considering such an approval. In fact, the deal eventually foundered over the problem of end user certificates, although North recommended emergency measures. On 10 June 1986, he wrote to Admiral Poindexter, 'we should look to going back to the head of an allied government on the blowpipes if we are going to do anything at all about outside support in the next few days, and I would love to carry the letter from RR [Ronald Reagan]'. Since Britain is the only 'allied government' which produces Blowpipes, these are grounds for believing that Mrs Thatcher knew of the deal.

Although the Tower Commission report contains evidence that Shorts may have taken part in an attempt to decieve the British Government over end use certificates, there has been no attempt to bring them to court, or apply special measures to their future export orders.

Esher's Oliver North

The bizarrely named Keeny Meeny Services (KMS) is the largest mercenary agency in Europe. Run by Major David Walker, KMS was 'set up predominantly to handle government work', according to a spokesman for its parent company, and sells paramilitary skills to governments and armies from Saudi Arabia to Sri Lanka. It has frequently been used by the Foreign Office to offer help to allied governments while preserving 'deniability'. KMS doesn't do anything important that his [Walker's] friends in Whitehall don't know about', explained one military source quoted in *The Daily News*.

Walker, a Cambridge engineer graduate and Tory councillor in the Esher backwater of Elmbridge, was described as a 'professional saboteur' by ◗

American States. It is situated on the Central American isthmus, an area unrelated to British defence needs. Yet until the Reagan administration turned Honduras into the 'Pentagon Republic', the British garrison was the witnesses in the Iran-contra hearings. On leaving the SAS in 1974, he helped establish KMS by bringing in other former SAS colleagues to provide bodyguards, helicopter pilots, special forces training and sabotage operations skills to a range of foreign governments. KMS made Walker a millionaire. A well known figure in the corridors of Whitehall, Walker is said to be 'on first name terms with the Prime Minister'. In 1982 he won a seat on the Elmbridge Borough Council, telling voters he was a 'keen sportsman and man of action'. He told friends he would one day like to be a Tory MP, an ambition that may have suffered from his recent spell in the spotlight.

Oliver North came to David Walker looking for training and sabotage operations. Walker originally persuaded him to fund a KMS strike on Soviet helicopters inside Nicaragua, but the deal collapsed amid recriminations between KMS men and the CIA commanders in charge of the operation. However, Walker did reportedly carry out an attack on the El Chipote arms depot in the centre of Managua in March 1985.

It is not known if anyone was killed in the attack. If so, the Labour Party's George Foulkes believes there is a clear case for prosecution for murder under Section 9 of the Offences Against the Person Act. Otherwise, he claims there is a case for a prosecution under the Foreign Enlistment Act, which makes it illegal for British subjects to take military action against a friendly country. So far there is no sign that any such charges are being considered.

When asked about KMS's role, Oliver North showed unusual reticence: 'I don't feel particularly comfortable discussing it in open session. I think there are equities that belong to other governments at stake here'. Once again, a tantalising glimpse of the Thatcher govenment's possible involvement in what was clearly more than a private gun-running operation.

The gunboat *Silver Sea*
The third case of a 'British connection' is the strange story of the *Silver Sea*, a 666-ton coaster which set sail from Southampton in February 1986, bound for Costa Rica and the contras, but only got as far as France before being impounded by the French authorities. John Collins, the Chief Officer of the ship, has testified that the vessel formed part of an operation to ship instalments of material worth £18 million to the contras, and that he had been told that the operation 'had the blessing of our own government'. The shipment, carrying mainly non-lethal military material such as jeeps and communications equipment, managed to evade customs clearance, again raising questions of a possible 'blind eye' from the authorities. Once again, no charges are to be brought over what an official investigation described as these 'minor irregularities'. According to reports in *The Observer*, the *Silver Sea* shipment was set up by Ronald Brennan, a British arms dealer, with money from the US.

largest permanent military presence of an external power in Central America.

The reason for this considerable British presence is the refusal of successive Guatemalan governments to recognise Belize's independence and their claim to sovereignty over all or parts of the country. Unlike virtually every other aspect of Mrs Thatcher's stance towards Latin America, her policy of maintaining British troops in Belize for an 'appropriate period' commands cross-party support. All the major political parties agree that the British military have to be there as a deterrent. The UK- and US-trained Belizean Defence Force (BDF), consisting of a maximum of 900 troops, would be no match for an invasion by the 40,000-strong Guatemalan army. Anachronistic as the policy may seem, progressive opinion both in the UK and Central America also supports the presence of the British troops. The most likely alternative – a US military force – would undoubtedly strengthen the US capacity to block much needed political and social change in the region.

In addition to the 1,800 troops, in 1987 the British deterrent force consisted of four Harrier jets, Puma and Gazelle helicopters, tanks and armoured personnel carriers, an air defence system based on Rapier missiles, and a Royal Navy frigate regularly patrolling the coast. The estimated cost to the British taxpayer in 1986 was around £31 million. But the net cost (ie if the cost of training the troops elswhere is deducted) was about £7 million, far lower than the commitment to the Falklands/Malvinas. Equally, if not more, important to the Belizeans is the contribution the British presence makes to the Belizean economy – perhaps as much as 25 per cent of Belize's national income. Some analysts suggest that the Belizean economy would actually collapse without the British garrison.

The Conservative government, like Labour governments before it, has always been keen to reduce or remove this commitment. The army is happy to go to Belize for the jungle and other military training it offers (it is also warmer than Germany and less dangerous than Northern Ireland). There is also a good public relations justification for its presence, in that it is suitably placed to respond quickly to natural disasters like the earthquakes in Mexico in September 1985 and El Salvador in October 1986. But the Treasury and most of the Ministry of Defence see its presence as an unreasonable expense when there are more pressing defence priorities in other areas of the world. The Foreign Office simply views it as an embarrassment in a post-colonial world. There are the added dangers that Britain may be dragged into the civil wars in Central America, an area which most Conservatives see as the 'natural concern' of the US, but not of Britain.

There is, however, little risk of Mrs Thatcher facing a repeat of the Falklands/Malvinas scenario in Belize. Despite the nationalist intransigence of the right in Guatemala, it is unlikely that the Guatemalan military would invade: their territorial ambitions were sobered by the British response to the Argentine invasion; the British defence force in Belize is stronger than in the Falklands/Malvinas prior to the invasion and more easily reinforceable; and Belize is a sovereign state and recognised by every country of the UN (including Argentina). Guatemala could count on virtually no international support if it invaded. It is far more likely that any shot fired by a British soldier in Belize would be connected with the increasing number of drug traffickers from the US and Colombia.

The main obstacle to any withdrawal is the difficulty of finding an agreement satisfactory to both Belize and Guatemala (see box). It is politically impossible for any Belizean government to cede territory, including cayes (coral reefs and sandbanks) off the Belizean coast, to Guatemala. But right-wing and military nationalists in Guatemala would probably not accept any agreement that did not include a cession of territory and/or the military use of some of the cayes.

The situation is complicated by international opposition to a withdrawal of British troops from Belize. The majority of Belizeans want them to stay for economic reasons and through a continual fear of the Guatemalan military – not just their territorial ambitions, but their reputation for ingrained racism and appalling brutality. Ironically, even a majority of Guatemalan officers are not too opposed to the British presence, as it acts as a buffer against the left-wing guerrilla group, the Rebel Armed Forces (FAR), which is active in the Petén, the department adjacent to Belize. Most significantly, the US wants Britain to stay: the soldiers act as a bulwark against the use of Belize as a possible conduit for arms to left-wing guerrillas in Guatemala or El Salvador (although there is no evidence of such traffic) and as a deterrent to drug traffickers using Belize as a conduit or a base; to have another external power in the region is useful to counter accusations of Central America being the sole concern of the US; Cuban influence could increase in the inevitable power vacuum after a British withdrawal; and the alternative of a US military presence could jeopardise US relations with the Guatemalan military.

Deals with Reagan?
On one highly publicised occasion, Mrs Thatcher seemed prepared to consider seriously a removal of troops against US wishes. A *Sunday Times* front-page story on 2 October 1983 claimed that in a private meeting with Reagan she had proposed a phased withdrawal from Belize. Although she later backtracked in the face of considerable US and backbench Conservative pressure, some British papers speculated that she may have made a deal with the Reagan administration, which may have included a lower price tag for the Trident nuclear missiles or an assurance of no US arms sales to Argentina.

Whatever deal may have been struck, she clearly did not want to upset the 'special relationship'. She has therefore been content to see the recent spectacular growth in the 'high intensity US peaceful domination' of Belize. This has included an increase in US diplomatic staff from 7 in 1981 to 47 in 1985, and 150 Peace Corps volunteers – per capita the largest Peace Corps presence in any country where they operate, despite Belize's small size. There is now 24-hour saturation of Belizean TV with US programmes; US

Negotiations

British involvement in what is now known as Belize started in the 17th century when British pirates established a settlement at the mouth of the Belize river in order to extract the rich timber in the surrounding area. The settlers successfully rebuffed frequent Spanish attempts to control the area. As a result, British Honduras, as it was later called, remained an English-speaking enclave throughout the 18th and early 19th centuries, and the most northerly member of a chain of British dependencies on the Caribbean coast of Central America.

Most Guatemalan maps still include Belize as an eastern department of Guatemala. Its claim is based on the assertion that it inherited sovereign rights over Belize at the time of its independence from Spain. Guatemala signed a border treaty with Britain in 1859 which was meant to settle the dispute, but later disavowed the pact when Britain failed to build a road between the Atlantic coast and Guatemala City, as stipulated in the agreement. The unbuilt road has since become, in the words of the Guatemala based weekly, *This Week*, 'the fig leaf for subsequent Guatemalan claims on the territory'. Guatemala has little, if any, international support for its claim. In 1980, 139 members of the UN General Assembly approved a resolution supporting Belize's rights and territorial integrity.

The nearest the three sides came to a settlement is said to be the so-called Heads of Agreement in March 1981, just six months before Belize's independence. It offered Guatemala free use of two oil pipelines, a road across Belize from the Petén to the Caribbean, the free use of two ports, and the 'use and enjoyment' of two cayes on the eastern approaches to the Caribbean Sea, together with an 8-mile sea lane into the open waters of the Caribbean. The ▶

personnel dictate and control Belizean drug control policy; there have been large increases in US economic and military aid; closer agreements with USAID on domestic economic policies such as pricing, trade and levels of public savings; and a Voice of America relay station has been established to step up propaganda against the Sandinista government.

Moreover, there are occasional rumours that Belize is being used as a staging-post for small arms going to the contras. In October 1986, for example, a C-130 plane, reportedly full of arms for the contras, was allegedly inspected by British troops and allowed to proceed. Reports have suggested that aircraft of Southern Air Transport, known to be a CIA front company, regularly stop off at Belize airport. The aircraft are known to carry 'confidential cargo' markings, and the head of Belize City airport has admitted that they are not searched.

Although suggestions that arms for the contras pass through Belize were corroborated in a Voice of America interview given by a contra representative in June 1986, the present conservative United Democratic Party (UDP) government of Belize has been quick to deny any involvement.

agreement collapsed after protests organised by the Belizean opposition United Democratic Party (which made it difficult for the UDP when in government to be seen to agree to anything resembling the Heads of Agreement), and more importantly, because both sides disagreed over what was meant by 'use and enjoyment'. To the Belizean Popular United Party (PUP) negotiators it meant Guatemalan tourists; to the Guatemalan military it meant some sort of a military, possibly radar, installation.

The next round of negotiations in January 1983 brought no advance. Belize again offered a slice of territorial waters, transit rights and a joint economic development programme but no territorial concessions, while the military government of Ríos Montt insisted on one-fifth of Belize (the department of Toledo). A great deal of optimism surrounded the latest round in April 1987, both because the new Guatemalan constitution of 1985 did not automatically include Belize as part of Guatemala, and because during a October 1986 visit to Europe Cerezo had expressed his willingness to 'recognise Belize's position'. But the Guatemalan team headed by Mario Quiñonez, the army's hard-line representative in the Guatemalan Foreign Office, merely reiterated Guatemala's desire for a chunk of Belize.

Most neutrals agree that a final settlement would have to consist of Guatemala dropping its claim to any territory in return for a sea corridor and economic aid, or a reworking of the 1981 Heads of Agreement. The present impasse would probably be allowed to simmer for some time, as a withdrawal of British troops suits no one but Britain. A victory by the Guatemalan left grouped in the URNG (National Revolutionary Unity of Guatemala) would almost certainly resolve the problem as they recognise Belize's independence and would drop all claims.

There are also frequent rumours of co-operation on military intelligence between British and Guatemalan officers (the new Brigadier in charge of the British forces is said to be an expert in counter-insurgency warfare), although this is virtually impossible to prove.

Thatcher and Guatemala
One of the major criticisms that can be made of Mrs Thatcher's policy towards the area is the speed with which the new Christian Democrat Guatemalan government of President Cerezo was welcomed by the British government. Between September 1981 and August 1986 there were no diplomatic relations between Britain and Guatemala as a result of the dispute over Belize. First consular, then full diplomatic, relations were restored in 1986 – moves which were seen by many as far too hasty a seal of approval for Cerezo's government at a time when nothing fundamental had changed within the country. Moreover, many Belizeans argued that the UK resumed relations without attempting to get some kind of concession from the Guatemalans on Belize. The Cerezo government was in fact very keen to

restore diplomatic relations in its search both for economic aid from the EEC and international acceptability after years of Guatemala being the pariah of the human rights world. It would have been a good moment to seek concessions.

Prior to Cerezo's government, Britain had consistently voted in favour of UN resolutions condemning Guatemala's appalling human rights record. Its stance was often at variance with that of the Reagan administration, which abstained, and was in contrast to its record of frequent abstentions during similar votes on Chile and El Salvador. Cynics explained the apparent inconsistency in terms of the British government's desire to have Guatemala portrayed in as bad a light as possible in the event of a Guatemalan military invasion of Belize. Britain's critical position changed after Cerezo's victory. In 1987, the UK voted in favour of the removal of the Special Rapporteur on Guatemala, despite a 1987 joint British Parliamentary Human Rights Group/AmericasWatch report that the human rights situation in Guatemala remained dismal. Furthermore, an offer of six 'technical scholarships' by Baroness Young was seen as more evidence of tacit approval of the new government.

An offical 'position paper' on Guatemala put out by the Foreign and Commonwealth Office (FCO) in 1987 confirmed the government's friendly disposition towards Cerezo. The December 1985 elections which Cerezo won were described as 'free and fair' when other observers pointed out the absence of serious candidates from the centre-left or left and the context of considerable fear and intimidation in which people voted. Cerezo was praised for his efforts to improve the human rights situation by dismantling the Department of Technical Investigations (DIT), setting up official bodies to monitor human rights and talking to the GAM (Mutual Support Group for the Disappeared). The paper failed to mention Amnesty International's concerns over continued killings and disappearances. The majority of the DIT officials were in fact rehired in other law-enforcement agencies, and only one officer was charged (with assault), while G-2, the military intelligence network, remained intact. Cerezo has failed to prosecute a single army officer for past atrocities, and there have been long delays in even forming a commission to investigate the disappeared in accordance with the demands of the GAM.

Privately, FCO officials have expressed warm admiration for Cerezo and the Christian Democrat option in Guatemala, which dovetailed neatly with its support for apparently 'moderate' options in El Salvador. In both countries, Christian Democrat governments were seen as preferable options to more radical change, despite the failure of both governments to address the root causes of the conflicts in both countries or to exert civilian control over the military, the main guarantors of the status quo.

The Caribbean: Britain bows out, the US steps in

In the context of the Caribbean, the 'special relationship' has functioned against a background of declining British influence and interest in the region. The Thatcher government inherited a long-standing policy of political and economic withdrawal from the Caribbean, and, like previous British governments, recognises US domination of the Caribbean as vital to the strategic interests of the Western alliance. With a steadily falling volume of Anglo-Caribbean trade, the Thatcher government has relatively few economic interests in the area. The colonial legacy is reduced to the defence commitment in Belize, an administrative responsibility in the few remaining dependencies and a more general and diplomatic role in the Commonwealth countries.

British policy in the Caribbean has almost invariably taken the form of uncritical support for US control of the region. In 1982, the government rejected the conclusions of a Foreign Affairs Committee report which recommended a more active and independent British role in the Caribbean, most notably in relations with Cuba and Grenada. Instead, the Thatcher government has consistently endorsed US regional policy and backed the Reagan administration's hostile response to non-capitalist development in the area. In collaboration with the US, Britain has assisted in the gradual militarisation of the Eastern Caribbean and the creation of a Regional Security Service, intended to counter drug smuggling and 'subversion'.

Grenada
The US theory of 'splashing dominoes' or communist infiltration of the Caribbean led to a severe, but short-lived, crisis in Anglo-American relations in 1983. Since March 1979, Washington had seen the People's Revolutionary Government (PRG) in Grenada as a threat to its regional interests. Following the example of the Callaghan government (which had blocked export licences for the sale of two armoured cars to the PRG), the Conservative administration adopted an antagonistic stance towards the former British colony and contributed to its economic destabilisation. Bilateral aid was cut from over £250,000 in 1979 and 1980 to £83,000 in 1981, and Grenada was excluded from a programme of emergency support following the hurricane damage of 1979 and 1980.

In accordance with the US policy of diplomatic isolation, Britain dutifully expressed its disapproval of the Grenadian revolution, accusing the regime of violating human rights and press freedoms and failing to hold elections, charges which were not levelled against such perceived allies as General Pinochet in Chile. According to Nicholas Ridley, then Minister of State at the Foreign Office: 'Grenada is in the process of establishing the kind of society of which the British government disapproves, irrespective of whether the people of Grenada want it or not'.

Until December 1983, British loyalty to the US view of the Grenadian 'threat' was unproblematic. In that month, however, as the PRG disintegrated in sectarian bloodshed and the Reagan administration seized its pretext for invasion, the 'special relationship' was seriously shaken. The invasion went ahead, despite British reservations and with a minimum of consultation, humiliating the Thatcher government and exploding the myth of partnership.

On the eve of the invasion, Sir Geoffrey Howe had assured the House of Commons that he knew of no intention to invade Grenada. Early the following morning, the Prime Minister had reportedly attempted to dissuade Reagan from military action. Later that afternoon, as Marines attacked the island, Howe was an easy target as Labour MPs accused him of incompetence and Mrs Thatcher of being the President's 'obedient poodle'. In the context of the debate over dual control of US Cruise missiles in the UK, Reagan's disregard of British wishes was potentially extremely damaging to the Conservative government.

Despite its embarrassment and anger, the British government neither condemned the invasion nor disputed the fabricated evidence which the Reagan administration produced to justify it. Instead, it assumed an equivocal position, distancing itself from the military action itself, but supporting the US in principle over its right to 'defend its citizens'. Mrs Thatcher's remarks reflected this ambiguity. On 27 October she asserted that the government stood by the US as 'the final guarantor of freedom in Europe'. On the 30th, however, she implicitly dissociated her government from the invasion, stating: 'when things happen in other countries which we don't like we don't just march in. We try to do it by persuasion.' Significantly, at no point did the British government question the constitutional illegality of what the US termed its 'rescue mission'. While every other European government condemned the invasion, Britain alone remained silent, abstaining in the subsequent UN vote of censure against the US action.

The invasion of Grenada caused considerable disarray within the Thatcher government and among Conservative MPs. Some felt that Britain should have assisted in or even led the military intervention, while others were violently opposed to the invasion. As the Queen was (and is) nominally the head of state in Grenada, the US action was interpreted by many as a violation of sovereignty and an insult to British standing in the region. What was altogether more dangerous to the Thatcher government, however, was the impression that the US was prepared to ignore British advice and pressure in the pursuit of its own foreign policy objectives.

Policing the Caribbean

The Grenada episode represented a temporary upset for the Thatcher/ Reagan alliance. Since then, however, the British stance of support for US policy in the Caribbean has remained unchanged. Events in Grenada have led to high level consultations on regional security, and in October 1984, Baroness Young announced that Britain was 'making arrangements to strengthen co-ordination with the United States, Canada and other Western partners'. British involvement has included military and police training for personnel from the Regional Security Service, participation in military exercises and financial support for coastguard facilities in the Eastern Caribbean. Aid to Grenada has been resumed, rising from £693,000 in 1984 to £1.45 million in 1985, and annual bilateral assistance of £25–30 million is available to friendly Caribbean governments.

In general, the Thatcher government fully supports the US 'free enterprise' approach towards the Caribbean's economic problems. Baroness Young indicated approval of Reagan's Caribbean Basin Initiative and expressed hopes that UK companies would be able to benefit from investment openings created by the programme. At the same time, the government has repeatedly stressed that Britain has its own priorities and its own historic links with the Caribbean. In a speech to the eighth Miami conference of Caribbean heads of state in 1985, Trade Minister Paul Channon reiterated that Britain 'had not lost interest in the Caribbean'.

In the wake of the Grenadian invasion and the growing militarisation of the region, there are many in the Caribbean who see British policy as indistinguishable from that of the US and who greet such statements with scepticism.

Chronology

1980

October   UK joins US in creation of a Caribbean regional coastguard, involving Barbados, St Lucia and St Vincent, aimed at countering 'potential threats of subversion' in the region

December   Britain abstains in vote at the UN General Asembly condemning El Salvador for human rights violations

1981

March   'Heads of Agreeement' talks between Britain and Guatemala over Belizean sovereignty collapse

September   Belize gains independence from Britain; Guatemala severs all diplomatic and commercial links with the UK in protest over sovereignty dispute

December   Britain abstains in UN General Assembly vote on human rights violations in El Salvador

1982

March   Britain is the only West European country to send official observers to the Salvadorean elections

December   British government expresses concern over renewal of US arms sales to Guatemala

               Britain attempts to exclude Nicaragua from an EEC aid package to Central America

1983

January   Talks with Guatemala break down after Guatemalan offer to drop its claim to all of Belize in return for the Toledo region (the southern fifth of the territory) is rejected

July   Foreign Office rejects claim by contra group, FDN, that talks with the British government are 'promising'; Sir Alfred Sherman, adviser to Mrs Thatcher, denies report that he is planning to visit El Salvador and Honduras to meet FDN representatives

October   US and token Caribbean force invades Grenada; Mrs Thatcher is criticised for failing to condemn the invasion

December   Britain abstains in UN General Assembly vote, condemning human rights situation in El Salvador

1984

March   Britain backs the US over the relocation of Salvadorean refugees in Honduras the British military attaché claims the move was necessary to prevent US military withdrawal from Europe

July   President Duarte of El Salvador meets UK government and is granted £100,000 in aid, technical assistance and postgraduate grants

September   Britain provides radio equipment, worth EC$2.1 million, for six Eastern Caribbean police forces

October   The UK government offers to train Salvadorean army officers at British bases in Belize

Leaked documents reveal shift in policy towards El Salvador; Britain now follows the US in backing loans for El Salvador from the World Bank and IDB

Britain announces intention to play a major role in security measures in the Caribbean; £1.5 million granted for coastguard shore facilities.

1985

January   Britain offers training places in UK to Salvadorean military

April   Conservative MP Winston Churchill visits Washington to petition Congress for aid to the contras

May   Britain supports US against Nicaraguan complaint in GATT over trade embargo

June   Senior officials from the Foreign Office meet contra leader Arturo Cruz

July   British military exercise *Jumping Mercury* takes place in the Caribbean, off the Turks and Caicos Islands

September   Britain participates in US wargame *Operation Exotic Palm*, designed to refine military technique in post-Grenada Caribbean

October   The Queen visits Belize

December   Britain votes in UN General Assembly to condemn human rights violations in El Salvador

1986

February   Britain condemns El Salvador in UN Human Rights Commission vote

July	Britain imposes direct rule in Turks and Caicos Islands, following allegations of official involvement in drugs trade and other corruption
August	Consular relations restored between Britain and Guatemala
December	Diplomatic relations restored between Britain and Guatemala

1987

January	Salvadorean military cadet commences 8-month training course at Sandhurst
March	US intelligence officials claim that Mrs Thatcher gave preliminary approval for sale of Blowpipe anti-aircraft missiles to the CIA, destined for the contras
	George Foulkes MP claims that Mrs Thatcher held meeting with Lieutenant-Colonel Oliver North and former head of CIA William Casey on Nicaraguan situation the preceding year
April	Tripartite talks between Britain, Belize and Guatemala break down after Guatemalan Foreign Minister, Mario Quiñonez, insists on Belize ceding part of its territory
May	Mrs Thatcher refuses to give categorical assurance that Britain was not involved in supplying arms to the contras, appealing to secrecy of intergovernmental communications
July	New moves announced between British, US and Caribbean governments to combat drugs-related activity in the Caribbean

4. Birds of a feather: Britain and Chile

The military coup in Chile in 1973 had an enormous impact on many people in Britain. Condemnation was wide-ranging, whether from those on the left who had sympathised with the efforts of the *Unidad Popular* (UP) government of Salvador Allende to introduce major social and political reforms in Chile or from those who were simply opposed to the destruction of the democratic system and horrified by the repression which followed the UP's overthrow.

Two years later, public awareness about the situation in Chile reached a household level in Britain with the news that a British doctor, Sheila Cassidy, had been arrested and brutally tortured by the DINA, the Chilean secret police. Combined with the considerable momentum that had built up in the broad labour movement for tougher action against the regime, the outrage generated by this incident led the Labour government to take strong measures. It broke off diplomatic relations with the Pinochet regime at ambassadorial level and imposed an embargo on arms sales to Chile. Attention was drawn to other human rights cases with a British connection, most notably that of the 'disappeared' Anglo-Chilean businessman and British passport holder, William Beausire. Beausire was detained at the end of 1974 and last seen in a torture centre in Chile in mid-1975. From the very beginning, the mistreatment of British citizens in Chile meant that Britain's diplomatic relations with the military regime were related to the human rights situation in Chile.

Britain was not alone in these years in condemning the Pinochet regime. The systematic violation of human rights and the absence of any real moves towards a return to democracy isolated the dictatorship in the arena of international diplomacy. However, this was not the case in the banking and financial world. Throughout the 1970s, the regime enjoyed the almost unconditional support of the international banking community and world financial institutions such as the IMF and World Bank. They offered crucial support for the regime's monetarist economic model, and in this way helped it to consolidate politically.

The sympathy of these institutions for Chile's economic restructuring was echoed by Mrs Thatcher when she came to office in Britain in 1979. Since then she has done everything possible to restore relations between the two countries, constrained only by the fact that Pinochet's arbitrary exercise of power and constant recourse to repression of dissent has never made such a policy unproblematic.

The 'normalisation' of relations, 1979—81

The direct link between British foreign policy and human rights was something that the incoming Conservative government sought to ignore from the outset. Full Export Credit Guarantee Department (ECGD) cover for business with Chile was restored in June 1979, and funding for the special refugee programme administered by the Joint Working Group for Refugees from Latin America ended in October on the grounds that 'there was no longer a demand'.

The next indication of the government's complete indifference to the human rights question came in January 1980 with the reinstatement of the British ambassador in Santiago – a move that was received with glee by the Pinochet regime. In other circumstances, the protestations of the Minister of State at the Foreign Office, at that time Nicholas Ridley, that the presence of an ambassador did not necessarily constitute a sign of approval, might have been plausible. But in the particular case of Chile, given the direct link between the previous withdrawal of the ambassador and human rights, this was little more than a sophism. Indeed, as was pointed out in an editorial of *The Times* (18 January 1980), far from being a neutral act, the restoration of full diplomatic relations was a sign of goodwill towards the military regime and a clear signal that the human rights situation was now of negligible concern to the British government. Furthermore, Ridley went so far as to suggest in February 1980 that Sheila Cassidy might have been wrong when she accused the Chilean secret police of torturing her.

The British government's cynical disregard for the violation of human rights in Chile was graphically illustrated by the bitterly controversial events that surrounded decision to lift the arms embargo. In announcing the decision to the Commons on 22 July 1980, Ridley claimed that the government had given the matter 'careful consideration' and defended the decision on the grounds that there had been 'a considerable improvement' in the human rights situation in Chile.

Yet only days earlier, on 16 July, Claire Wilson, an Anglo-Chilean student, had been arrested, tortured and pressed to give up her British citizenship by the security forces. The British Embassy intervened to help secure her release on 18 July, but it failed to question her about allegations of torture. On 22 July, the day the arms embargo was lifted, the Embassy received a copy of a *habeas corpus* writ outlining her mistreatment. Ridley was later to claim (when the press began to uncover details of the affair in September) that he had been unaware of its existence at the time of the Commons announcement. For its part, the Embassy also claimed to have been unaware that the British government planned to lift the arms embargo on 22 July and it was only a week later that the Claire Wilson case was eventually raised with the Chilean authorities.

Not surprisingly, commentators were quick to conclude that the British government had deliberately withheld information from Parliament that could have affected the Commons debate on the lifting of the arms embargo. At the very least, the apparent lack of communication between the Foreign Office and the British Embassy made a mockery of the justification for the reinstatement of the ambassador in Santiago that had been given by Ridley only months earlier: 'We have used our ambassadors wherever appropriate or necessary to follow up particular cases involving human rights in a large number of countries: this is an important reason for having an ambassador in Chile. . . . When it comes to human rights, this government prefers action to words.'

Impervious to the furore surrounding the lifting of the arms embargo, the British government then despatched the Trade Minister, Cecil Parkinson, on a mission to Chile (and – ironically, given subsequent events – to Argentina) in August 1980. The following year, the ex-Royal Navy County Class Destroyer, HMS *Norfolk* and the tanker, HMS *Tidepool* were sold to Chile despite protests that the military government had used naval vessels as torture centres after the coup.

Having 'normalised' bilateral relations between Britain and Chile, the Thatcher government then moved to provide aid to the Pinochet regime in international fora. For the first time since the coup, the government refused to condemn the regime's human rights record in a United Nations body and abstained on the resolution submitted to the UN Commission for Human Rights in February 1981 on the grounds that the treatment of Chile in the UN was 'selective' and that the regime's critics displayed 'imbalance'.

International solidarity of the 'new right'

The determination with which the British government helped the regime, despite its treatment of British citizens, not to mention the Chilean people, raises a number of questions. It was clearly much more than a case of the Tories reversing on 'technical' grounds the 'excessive' policies of the previous Labour government. Indeed, it should be seen within the context of the global offensive of the 'new right' and therefore as a sympathetic act of 'solidarity', based on common ideological ground.

An outstanding feature of the rhetoric of both the Thatcher government and the Pinochet regime is its almost identical ideological foundation. As political scientist Philip O'Brien has written, the two governments share 'the anti-statism, pro-free market "monetarist" prescriptions associated with the new orthodoxy/Chicago school of Milton Friedman and Friedrich von Hayek on the economic side, and the cold war, national security, right-wing populist rhetoric emphasizing law and order, religion, race, family, chauvinism and anti-welfarism on the political side'. In this sense, a crucial element in the military regime's economic programme has been its role as a laboratory or testing ground for the subsequent introduction of free market policies by conservative governments in many industrialised countries.

Many members of the Thatcher government have explicitly admired the military regime's vanguard role in adopting a radical monetarist economic model and have not shied away from projecting the Chilean experience onto their own. As stated by Cecil Parkinson in *El Mercurio* (2 November 1980) following his visit to Chile: 'The Chilean economic experience is very similar to what we are developing here [in Britain]'. In December 1982, one of Mrs Thatcher's main economic advisers at the time, Alan Walters, visited Chile for a ten day visit in which he held talks with Pinochet and his economic team.

Obvious differences exist between the two monetarist experiments (e.g. economic structure, differing levels of repression, depth of privatisation, Chile's inferior position in the international economic order, etc.). Neverthless, so many similarities do exist that the drawing of parallels is useful. These include increased state control over the operation of trade unions and restrictions on the collective strength of the union movement; increased police powers and restrictions on the right to assembly; the maintenance of a permanent core of unemployed (many of whom, like youth, have never worked before); the existence of short term unemployment schemes as a source of cheap labour; moves to bring the education system in line with the new economic order; the deliberate engineering of a slump (Britain 1980–2, Chile 1975–6) with which to rationalise the economy and prepare the ground for long-term economic and social restructuring; the increased opening of the economy to the international market and the penetration of foreign capital; the shift in favour of the finance and services sector to the detriment of manufacturing industry; the erosion of the welfare state and moves towards its privatisation. What is already an extensive list could easily be further developed.

In considering the Thatcher government's ideological affinity with the policies of the Pinochet regime, the importance that the defeat of the UP experiment in 1973 represented for the capitalist class worldwide cannot be underestimated. The efforts of the UP government to implement an ambitious programme of structural reforms aimed at paving the way for the 'democratic transition to socialism' had a political impact that transcended national boundaries. The fact that the socialist 'transformation' was to take form gradually within the framework of the existing institutional system (and not as a result of a violent break) was seen by many on the European left as an experiment of key historical significance, relevant to potentially similar projects in their own countries.

Obviously the relevance of the UP experience varied from country to country. In Britain, the emergence of a socialist alternative designed to overcome the contradictions of the post-war consensus was never seriously on the agenda. Nevertheless, the 1970s did see a number of victories by the labour movement. Episodes such as the miners' defeat of the previous Heath government were not taken lightly by British capital. Thus, just as a central theme of Pinochet's discourse has been that Keynesian-style interventionism in the economy and the 'demagogic politics' of the Allende years had harboured the seeds of 'marxist totalitarianism', much of Mrs Thatcher's invective against the social democratic post-war consensus has been based on the idea that it is the root cause of economic stagnation, the breakdown of law and order, and overall national decline.

Military co-operation and the 'Falklands factor'

Relations between the British government and the Pinochet regime entered a new phase in the wake of the war with Argentina in the South Atlantic in 1982. Now, considerations of military strategy and geo-political concerns gave Britain an additional interest in further strengthening its links with the regime. In such a situation, the scant importance that the British government had previously attached to the issue of human rights was reduced even further.

Along with the *Belgrano* affair, it is believed that the specific details regarding the military co-operation between Britain and Chile (and the mutual favours that resulted) were among the most sensitive subjects of the Falklands/Malvinas war and were classified as top secret. The Ministry of Defence was alarmed by the number of press leaks about the Chile connection and the 'D-Notice Committee' was instructed to ensure that nothing was reported. According to the *New Statesman* (25 January 1985), news editors were warned that the issue was 'sensitive' and were asked not to mention it.

Co-operation between Britain and Chile began from the outbreak of the war. Within a week a number of secret understandings had been arranged between the British Embassy in Santiago and the Pinochet regime. These were set out in top secret telegrams from the British Embassy in Santiago to the Foreign Office in London, stating that co-operation with Britain had gained the approval of General Pinochet and his cabinet. The agreement stipulated that in return for the use of Chilean military bases and intelligence during the war, Britain was to provide the regime with military equipment and to 'lay off' Chile over human rights issues.

The first part of Britain's secret operation from Chile came in mid-April when a number of Canberra PR9 spy planes were flown to Belize to be repainted in Chilean Air Force markings and then continue their flight to an airbase near Punta Arenas in southern Chile. From there, the Canberras undertook spy missions to the three main airbases in southern Argentina, Río Grande, Río Gallegos and Ushuaia, which were located a mere 160 miles away. Top RAF intelligence expert Group Captain David L. Edwards liaised directly with General Fernando Matthei, Commander-in-Chief of the Chilean Air Force and member of the military junta.

The second part of the operation was the setting up of a base near Punta Arenas for the launching of SAS raids into Argentina. Of particular importance was the raid on 20 May on the Río Grande airbase, which disabled several Exocet-carrying Super Etendard aircraft just before the British task force landed on the Falklands. The SAS operations had nearly been exposed only days earlier when a Royal Navy Sea King helicopter was forced to land between Punta Arenas and Dawson Island in Chile. Throughout the conflict Chilean naval intelligence was also important for the interception of Argentine military and navy radio signals.

The Pinochet government began to receive its pay-off from Britain immediately. In April and May 1982, eight Hawker Hunter ground attack aircraft were donated to the regime, and a further consignment of four left for Chile in January 1983. In line with the secret agreement, it is believed that as many as six of the RAF Canberra aircraft used in the spy mission over Argentina were also turned over to the Pinochet regime by the end of 1982. Such was the flow of military equipment to Chile at this time that the Chilean Air Force even set up a depot at Luton airport.

A further sign of the growing warmth of military relations was the visit to Britain in September 1982 of General Herman Brady, head of the Chilean Nuclear Energy Commission, who met the UK Atomic Energy Authority and was offered a British magnox nuclear reactor. Forty enriched uranium fuel rods were sent to Chile for work in the Lo Aguirre research reactor. The following year members of the military junta came to Britain for the first time. General Matthei, Commander-in-Chief of the Chilean Air Force, arrived in March 1983. He had cancelled a previous visit in August 1982, following Labour and Alliance protests at his invitation to the Farnborough Air Show by the Society of British Aerospace Companies. Although the British government insisted that Matthei's visit was a 'private' affair, he was personally thanked for the regime's help during the war by the RAF Chief of Staff, Air Marshal Sir Keith Williamson. Then, in June 1983, the head of the Chilean Navy, Admiral José Toribio Merino included Britain in a tour of Europe.

The flourishing of relations between the British government and the Pinochet regime in the wake of the South Atlantic conflict was perhaps most eloquently expressed by the then Trade Minister, Peter Rees, during a British trade delegation to Santiago in September 1982. Speaking on the ninth anniversary of the coup, Rees referred to the military government as 'a moderating and stabilising force in Latin America' with which Britain was 'interested in deepening and strengthening political relations' (*Observer*, 12 September 1982).

Human rights 'trade off'

One of the most important of the British government's moves to aid the Pinochet regime has been its efforts to undermine the monitoring by the United Nations of human rights abuses in Chile and relieve the regime of a constant source of embarrassment. In the UN General Assembly in December 1982 the British government lobbied for support for an amendment it had presented in the Third Committee to a draft resolution condemning repression in Chile. This would have meant putting an end to the UN General Assembly's annual practice of making strong recommendations for the renewal of the mandate of the Special Rapporteur (and thus the continued provision of reports on the situation in Chile) and leaving such a decision to the UN Commission on Human Rights on an ad hoc basis.

This move delighted the Pinochet regime. It aimed to downgrade the treatment of the Chilean case in the UN from a permanent airing to the nations of the world in the more 'public' and 'political' forum of the General Assembly, to the more limited and 'technical' framework of the 43-nation Commission on Human Rights. Indeed, the amendment was a clear step towards the eventual elimination of the Special Rapporteur. However, in spite of its approval in the Third Committee, the amendment was overturned in the plenary of the General Assembly and, at this stage, the British government, unhappy at seeing its manoeuvre foiled, abstained in the final vote.

The British government was now deliberately distorting the facts concerning the Pinochet regime's human rights record. It used the benchmark of 1977 instead of the true yardstick of the pre-1973 situation in order to claim in 1982 that there had been an improvement in the human rights situation in Chile. There had, in fact, merely been a change in the nature of human rights abuses. Individual extra-judicial deaths, short-term arrest and the permanent use of torture had replaced mass killings and regular 'disappearances'.

In 1983, in spite of the fact that comparative statistics for the 1982–3 period revealed a quadrupling of killings and cases of torture and an eight-fold increase in political arrests, the British government asserted that the Chilean government had been taking 'positive steps' to improve its human rights record. Rejecting suggestions that 'improvements' (a temporary reduction in press censorship and permission for some exiles to return to Chile) were merely cosmetic, the British government once again abstained in the vote on Chile in the UN General Assembly in 1983.

The British government was indifferent when it came to concrete action and encouragement for those in Chile defending human rights, or intervention in individual cases of repression. Human rights leaders in Chile complained that, unlike other embassies (even those sympathetic to the regime, such as the US), the British Embassy maintained irregular contact, would not make enquiries when serious human rights cases arose, and would not comment on reports. Such neglect also extended to those human rights cases with a British connection. Two secret police agents, who had been identified by witnesses as being responsible for the torture of William Beausire, had been located in 1982. But the British government made no effort to follow this up, and after denials by the two agents concerned, the military courts were allowed to shelve the case in 1983. Astonishingly, the Foreign Office justified its lack of action on the grounds that there was no new evidence in the case.

Despite all such criticisms, the British government has always maintained publicly that it is concerned with the defence of human rights in Chile. However, the extent to which such assurances have been manufactured for public consumption was revealed by internal Foreign Office documents, leaked in mid-1985 (*Chile Fights*, Summer 1985). While these 'Contingency Planning' documents confirmed what was in many ways already common knowledge, they provided written proof of the remarkable duplicity with which the British government has presented its relations with the Pinochet regime. The Thatcher government had always rejected charges that it lacked the political will to bring effective pressure to bear on Pinochet, and persistently defend its policy of 'quiet diplomacy' on the grounds that the more vigorous diplomatic gestures advocated by its critics would be unproductive. The leaked documents told another story:

> an arms embargo . . . would be a striking political gesture on our behalf. But it would also carry unacceptable penalties. The Chileans would regard an embargo as a major shift in British policy; and this could, in turn, hazard the defence and other cooperation that we enjoy over the Falklands. . . . Whilst a recall [of the ambassador] would be an effective way of demonstrating our concern to the Chileans, the danger is that it could, in turn, provoke appetites in Parliament for a more substantial scaling down of our relations with Chile.

One of the most worrying features of the documents was their attitude to arms sales to Chile. Officially the Thatcher government has claimed that it would not supply equipment that could be used for internal repression and that the sale of arms could not be interpreted as an endorsement of the regime's policies. However, the reference in the documents to the possible sale of 300 gun-carrying Centaur military vehicles as 'politically contentious' and 'to be watched carefully' unmistakably suggested that the government was prepared to sell such equipment in spite of its awareness of its repressive capabilities.

Political change and policy shifts

British policy towards Chile during the Thatcher years has been projected onto a situation which is far from static. With the forceful emergence of political opposition to the Pinochet regime, events in Chile have developed in a dramatic way and this has meant that bilateral relations have become more complex. While 1982–4 was undoubtedly the period of maximum co-operation between Mrs Thatcher and the Pinochet regime, the deepening crisis of the military government from that time onwards forced the British government to re-examine its policies. Until mid-1983 the British Embassy's range of contacts in the opposition and human rights field was limited to the absolute minimum. However, from this time on, it gradually began to build bridges with representatives of the moderate opposition.

On closer examination, Britain's attitude to the internal political situation in Chile reveals remarkable parallels with that of its senior partner in the 'new cold war', the Reagan administration. Like the US, the British government is anxious to avoid moves that might destabilise the Pinochet regime and thus favour a divided, but still influential left. However, while control of the left may be an overriding consideration, the Reagan and Thatcher governments have also been worried at the way in which Pinochet's intransigence has often dangerously polarised the Chilean situation. While unconditional support to Pinochet might at one time have caused no problems, they have gradually come to believe that the military government under his leadership cannot guarantee long-term stability in the country.

Like the US, Britain has therefore followed a two-pronged strategy. On the one hand, it has pushed for an agreement between the 'moderate' opposition ,represented by the centrist *Alianza Democrática* (AD), dominated by the Christian Democrat party) and the political right which until recently gave unconditional support to the regime. On the other hand, it has sought to strengthen the position of the 'moderates' within the regime and the armed forces in order to build a bridge with the centre-right. The aim has been to press for a modification of the conditions under which the Pinochet government operates, paving the way for an 'orderly' transition *from within the military's existing constitutional framework* to a 'liberalised', restricted political system by 1989 (when Pinochet's current term in office comes to an end). In this way, the basic tenets of the regime would remain essentially intact, and the left would either be excluded outright, or forced to accept the terms of the transition and a very weak position in the country's political future.

This task has not been an easy one. Only days after hundreds of people had been shot dead or wounded in protests, the British government backed the regime's announcement in August 1983 of an *apertura* (political opening, political liberalisation) in the country. It expressed its confidence that the regime would bring forward the introduction of its 'political laws' contemplated in the constitution, permitting limited political activity by non-marxist parties. It also actively encouraged the limited talks that subsequently took place between the centrist opposition and the regime.

However, the 'dialogue', as it came to be known, broke down and the gradual hardening of the regime throughout 1984 ruled out its resumption. Political confrontation intensified sharply throughout 1984, culminating in a two-day protest led by the left at the end of October which paralysed the country. A fierce wave of repression accompanied the imposition of a state of siege on 6 November.

The violent interruption of the *apertura* caused consternation in Whitehall. In response, Sir Geoffrey Howe held a meeting in December 1984, in which various policy options were discussed. The meeting was to prepare for a further deterioration in the situation in Chile. It was to this discussion that the leaked Foreign Office 'Contingency Planning' documents were presented. According to the documents, the meeting considered a range of possible pressures against the military government, including various diplomatic measures and limited economic sanctions, such as instructing the British delegation at the World Bank or the Inter-American Development Bank to block loans to Chile. This did not necessarily mean that a fundamental shift had taken place in British policy or that the Thatcher government was now contemplating measures designed to weaken the regime. Instead, it was a recognition that some pressure might be needed to keep the regime on the rails of a gradual centre-right transition and to ensure that the ambitions of one individual did not jeopardise the whole system.

The seriousness with which the Thatcher government viewed the situation was also reflected in other ways. After the cynical manoeuvring of the previous years, in 1984 Britain was forced to return to the policy of voting in favour of human rights condemnations in the UN – a position that has grudgingly been maintained since. In February 1985, Sir William Harding, Under-secretary of State for the Americas at the Foreign Office, was sent to Santiago where he met with Pinochet, government ministers, the parties of the centre and right and – a noteworthy step forward – human rights and trade union organisations. Although he kept a guarded silence about the conversation with Pinochet, Harding is reported to have expressed his concern in several meetings that Chile could become 'another Nicaragua' and the focus for East-West conflict.

Such cold war analysis had been an even greater feature during the visit of Harding's counterpart from the US State Department, Assistant Secretary for Inter-American Affairs Langhorne Motley, only a week earlier. Harding dismissed any link between the two visits. However, once again, it is impossible not to find some degree of symmetry between the initiatives of the US and British governments. Britain's contingency planning and the decision to send an envoy followed hot on the tracks of an earlier policy review on Chile by the Reagan administration involving the State Department, the Treasury, the Pentagon and the CIA.

In the wake of the state of siege (November 1984–June 1985), reports indicated that the US, Britain and West Germany had agreed on a joint policy. This was to allow Pinochet to run his full term until 1989 but also to ensure that the situation would be fully 'normalised' in preparation for the possible disappearance of the regime *in its current form* beyond 1989. Ironically, in spite of its negative effects, the state of siege played a significant role in creating conditions for such a project to take concrete shape. Given the degree of repression, all sectors of the opposition, but particularly the political centre, emerged from the state of siege weakened and with lower expectations.

It was in such circumstances that the 'National Accord for a Transition to Full Democracy', sponsored by the hierarchy of the Catholic Church, emerged in August 1985. Based principally on an alliance between the AD and the right wing, the 'Accord' also drew some support from the centre-left. It excluded a sizeable chunk of the left, represented by the marxist *Movimiento Democrático Popular* (MDP, whose main force is the Communist Party). The initiative received support from a broad spectrum of opinion, including social democratic and socialist parties in Western Europe (the British Labour Party among them).

It is not difficult, however, to see why Britain and the US viewed the 'Accord' as a step in the 'right' direction. The proposals of the 'Accord' for the future socio-economic framework were unmistakably right of centre. They provided certain guarantees to the armed forces over possible sanctions on human rights abuses. The 'Accord' implicitly suggested that Pinochet would have to go and favoured open presidential elections, but it also foresaw a gradual transition from within the existing constitutional framework by 1989 rather than an immediate break with the military government and its policies and institutions. The 'Accord' thus provided a considerable degree of compatibility with the 'moderate' sections of the regime and members of the latter, such as junta member General Matthei, openly welcomed this fact.

Given the strategic aims of the British government, one of the main questions at present, of course, is what stance it will adopt towards the succession to Pinochet in 1989. According to the regime's constitution, the heads of the armed forces must nominate a presidential candidate who will then be approved in a national referendum and rule for an eight-year period until 1997 in a 'protected democracy'. Until the crisis of the regime, it had always been assumed that the candidate would be Pinochet, but the considerable array of forces stacked against his renomination for a second term means that this is no longer necessarily the case. Indeed, it would appear that the British government is already making preparations. Both immediately before and after Mrs Thatcher's victory in the general election of June 1987, three of the four members of the military junta (the head of the military police, Rodolfo Stange; the head of the navy, Admiral Merino; and the head of the air force, General Matthei) – who have all strongly implied that they do not want to see Pinochet as the candidate – visited Britain. Merino held talks with Tim Eggar, Under-secretary of State at the Foreign Office.

In view of the Thatcher government's commitment to a transition within the framework of the regime's own constitution and its desire to exclude the left (in particular Chile's powerful Communist Party), it is evident that the British government will do little to press for free and open elections. Instead, it seems more likely that the Thatcher government will opt for a replacement for Pinochet in a single candidate plebiscite; or, failing this, a limited two-way competition between a candidate of the centre-right and one put forward by the armed forces. As experience has shown, the restoration of pluralistic democracy in Chile is not the British government's aim; rather it is the introduction of a restricted political system that would continue to live under the shadow of military tutelage.

Chronology

1979

June	Export credit guarantees restored for UK business with Chile
October	Government ends funding for special programme of Joint Working Group for Refugees from Latin America

1980

January	British government restores full diplomatic relations with Chile after a break of four years.
July	British Embassy delays gaining release of British subject Claire Wilson from detention and torture in a Chilean jail
	Arms embargo lifted
August	Trade Minister Cecil Parkinson visits Chile and Argentina

1981

February	Britain abstains in UN Human Rights Commission vote on Chile
September	Senior Chilean naval officers attend the Royal Navy Equipment Exhibition in Portsmouth, resulting in the sale of two Royal Navy ships

1982

April(?)	Secret deal between Thatcher and Pinochet governments agrees Chilean support for UK in Falklands/Malvinas conflict in return for arms and diplomatic assistance
August	General Fernando Matthei, head of Chilean Air Force and junta member, cancels visit to Farnborough Air Show as a result of protests
September	Peter Rees, Trade Minister, declares Chile 'a moderate and stabilising force in South America', while leading a trade delegation to Santiago
	General Brady, head of Chilean Nuclear Energy Commission, meets UK Atomic Energy Authority and is offered a British reactor and other equipment
November	Sir Francis Pym tells the House of Commons: 'Chile was quite helpful to us in the [Falklands/Malvinas] conflict and we ought to bear that in mind when we consider our relations with her now'
December	UK abstains on a vote in the UN General Assembly condemning Chile for human rights violations
	Alan Walters, economic adviser to the government, visits Chile

1983

March	General Matthei visits Britain and is thanked for military assistance during Falklands/Malvinas campaign
June	Toribio Merino, Chief of Chilean Navy and junta member, visits London for talks with Ministry of Defence and Admiralty
December	UK abstains in UN General Assembly vote condemning human rights violations in Chile

1984

January	Department of Trade and Industry issues export licence for armed Centaur military vehicles
February	Visit to Chile by members of Conservative Party Bow Group
March	Chilean Finance Minister Carlos Caceres visits UK to negotiate repayment of debt
December	Sir Geoffrey Howe holds meeting to consider UK government's contingency options on changing situation in Chile
	Britain votes to condemn Chile in UN General Assembly debate on human rights

1985

February	Executive Director of Chilean Nuclear Energy Commission visits UK
June	'Contingency Planning' documents leaked and published
July	12 Chilean officers from National Academy of Political and Strategic Studies visit UK as guests of Ministry of Defence
	Chilean Finance Minister Hernan Buchi addresses meeting of creditor banks in London as guest of Midland Bank
December	Britain votes in the UN to condemn human rights violations in Chile

1986

October	Hernan Somerville, senior official of Chilean Central Bank, visits London to discuss debt renegotiation with Midland Bank
November	IMF votes to disburse US$250 million loan to Chile. US abstains; Britain votes in favour

1987

May	General Matthei visits UK as part of European tour to secure arms deals
June	Rodolfo Stange, head of Chilean Military Police, visits UK
July	Admiral Merino visits UK

5. 'A small colonial war': the Falklands/Malvinas dispute

A few hours before he was inaugurated as the new president of Argentina in December 1983, Raúl Alfonsín decided to allow me to interview him for the *Observer*. In the intimate environment of the small hotel room he was occupying at the time, Alfonsín confided that his maternal grandmother came from a British backround and was called Foulkes, and that he looked forward to shaking hands with Mrs Thatcher. 'A fundamental argument that used to be held by people in Britain as a reason for not negotiating with us has now disappeared. We are no longer a de facto regime, nor are we run by a dictatorship. We Argentines have finally understood that we will always be a tin-pot country if we don't follow a golden rule: the armed forces must come under the firm control of the civilian powers', Alfonsín said.

The president's remarks sprang from an accurate assessment of what from the Argentine side had contributed to the outbreak of the Falklands war in 1982. The invasion of the islands was an offensive act by an unelected and bloody military regime which exploited an essentially emotional and irrational concept of cultural identity behind the myth of national unity. Subsequently the war showed the terrifying ease with which militarism inflates a nationalist ego and breeds a distorted perception of the rest of the world.

And yet even at this close range, with so many of the central issues still unresolved, one can see how self-deluded Alfonsín was about the nature of Thatcherism and its implications for Falklands policy both before, during, and since the war.

This chapter will not attempt to give a blow-by-blow account of military and diplomatic events preceding and during the Falklands war, on which there is already an extensive bibliography published in both Britain and Argentina. But a limited backround is necessary to provide the context for developments since the war and to support the view that Mrs Thatcher's role in the Falklands issue has already shown itself to be a great deal more complex than many of her more vehement supporters or detractors make out.

The military momentum

The Falklands crisis illustrated first and foremost how easily the concept of national sovereignty can, given particular political circumstances, lead inevitably to war. From a historical perspective, it has become increasingly clear that the relative rights and wrongs of the rival claims to the islands are largely irrelevant when explaining the main event. The key lies in the extent to which sovereignty was exploited by either side.

Evidence supplied in Buenos Aires since the end of the war has demonstrated beyond doubt that Argentina's military junta began to draw up an invasion of the islands from the end of 1981 onwards. Prior to this there had been instances of draft occupation plans secretly prepared by successive military governments and of at least one clandestine commando expedition to the islands. Within Argentina the period from mid-1981 to early 1982 was characterised by growing internal political unrest, largely on account of the junta's mismanagement of the economy.

Prior to April 1982, there is no record of a single major demonstration in Argentina in support of the seizure of the islands, and even the occasional attacks on British property and two public 'landings' by nationalist civilians had failed to generate widespread excitement on the mainland. And yet the Malvinas had historically featured in school curricula, and were remembered in street names and national days. They were less important in themselves as a nationalist myth, a potentially dangerous therapy for a frustrated country in search of an identity.

Much has been written about the military failings of the British government in those crucial first three months in 1982. But it is only one of many paradoxes of the Falklands story that these 'failings' stemmed not from the resolute approach with which Thatcherism is popularly identified now, but from the Prime Minister's lack of it. Her failure to send a dissuasive force of nuclear submarines at the beginning of March 1982, her continuing tendency to discount evidence of increased tension and rumours of impending military action in Buenos Aires, her bungled and belated use of HMS *Endurance* (virtually recalled from its way to the scrap heap) in South Georgia, and her final inability to read the true intention of Admiral Anaya despite ample warning from the US are some instances of a serious lack of judgment.

Less attention has been paid to the ideological failings of British foreign policy which may have also contributed to tempting the junta to act the way it did. The broad outlines of contemporary British foreign policy as it has applied to the Falklands can be traced to the Duncan Report in the late 1960s. This essentially identified the North Atlantic Alliance and Western Europe as the main centres of military and political interest. Latin America, and particularly Argentina, was relegated effectively to its former 'colonised' status, where British ambassadors were instructed to co-operate with any regime that encouraged the purchase of British goods.

A context of indifference

With the exception of David Owen's short tenure at the Foreign Office, during which a British arms sale to Argentina was contested for political reasons, successive Labour and Conservative governments pursued similar policies towards Argentina and the Falklands: a low profile when it came to human rights violations; the pursuit of trade links, particularly defence contracts; and negotiations over the islands aimed at minimising tension between the islands and the mainland (and thus preserving British commercial interests) and focusing on the possible implementation of a lease-back agreement which would acknowledge Argentine claims to sovereignty, yet protect the rights and life-style of the kelpers.

With the election of the Thatcher government in 1979, British foreign policy towards Argentina and the Falklands changed in degree rather than substance. A month after taking office the government restored diplomatic relations with the junta which had been temporarily interrupted in 1976, when an economic and social survey of the islands undertaken by Lord Shackleton had led to tension with Buenos Aires, which demanded negotiations on the issue of sovereignty. In 1980 the junta's finance minister, José Martínez de Hoz, so befriended British banks that he was renamed 'the Wizard of Hoz' on a tour of Europe. The same year, Cecil Parkinson, then Minister of Trade, told parliament: 'I believe civil trade with other countries should be determined by commercial considerations and not by the character of the governments concerned'. The definition of what constituted 'civil trade' was left vague, allowing British arms dealers to pursue lucrative links with Buenos Aires. Equipment sold included type 42 destroyers, Seacat missile systems, Lynx naval helicopters, and small arms. This was accompanied by military training, exchange visits, and the loaning of military experts to Argentina.

The Committee of Privy Councillors that in January 1983 published its review (the Franks Report) on policy towards the Falklands in the period leading up to the invasion of 2 April, concluded by exonerating the Thatcher government of any blame for the event. But this conclusion contradicted the evidence that Mrs Thatcher could and should have acted sooner to avert war. Moreover, while the report chronicles in detail the military and diplomatic events behind the Falklands war, it makes little reference to the political developments within Argentina whose real meaning the Thatcher government overlooked through a process of misconceived diplomatic and commercial self-interest.

The fact that Operación Azul, the invasion programme, was planned and executed by a restricted group of military officers without the knowledge of the vast majority of the Argentine nation suggests that a key explanation for the war can be found in the militarised nature of Argentine political culture, in which Britain acquiesced while ignoring its wider implications. It should be noted in passing, moreover, that compared to the ignorance displayed by

British officialdom (and the total apathy of the mass of the British people), the islanders themselves showed a great deal more sensitivity to the real character of Argentine politics. To them the complacency of British officials contrasted with the harrowing reports about human rights violations made by the BBC's Buenos Aires correspondent, Derek Wilson. To listeners in London such reports seemed remote; the newspapers they read in the morning treated most of Latin America, Argentina included, as equally unimportant. But for the kelpers, living just two hours flying time away, the reports created an underlying psyche of fear and distrust. There is little evidence, judging by the lack of investment in the islands prior to the war, that even Mrs Thatcher really saw their feelings as something that should be taken into account.

Mixed motives

Anthony Barnett, in his analysis of the war (*Iron Britannia: Why Britain Waged its Falklands War*), has already provided a detailed and revealing account of Britain's initial reaction to the invasion and the way in which, with a few exceptions, MPs from all three major political groupings endorsed without qualification the sending of the task force. Barnett wrote of that memorable debate of 3 April when politician after politician lined up to beat the jingoistic drum, arguing the necessity of delivering the kelpers from the evil grip of the junta:

> In parliamentary terms, the pressure of this argument was very strong. It gave the Government no room for manoeuvre. 'We saved it, you have lost it, either you get it back or get out'. Had it been unemployment that was being debated, the rhetoric would be regarded as dull . . . but it was the nation's honour that was at stake, in a contest in which each party seeks to represent the nation, at the expense of the other.

From that moment – not prior to the invasion, as some have argued – Mrs Thatcher's political survival became inexorably linked with the Falklands issue. 'The figure of Margaret Thatcher towers over the Falklands drama from its inception to the euphoria of the final triumph', wrote Simon Jenkins and Max Hastings in *The Battle for the Falklands*. While Mrs Thatcher cannot escape her share of responsibility for the original debacle, the relative merits of her policy once the invasion had taken place are more open to argument.

Although the image that persists is of Mrs Thatcher completely convinced of the feasibility of sending a task force and remaining utterly tenacious, her actual position for most of the war was not without its contradictions. To say that Mrs Thatcher sought conflict eagerly and was cynical in the pursuit of peace disregards the deliberate slowing down of the task force to allow for more negotiations to take place and the compromises offered in good faith under the terms of the Peruvian and UN peace plans, compromises that represented substantive retreats from the government's initial promises to parliament. In purely historical terms, the argument that the sinking of the *General Belgrano* was in itself sufficient to destroy irrevocably any chance of peace does not stand up to investigation. Mrs Thatcher's detractors have failed to produce conclusive evidence that the sinking was a deliberate decision to scupper the Peruvian peace initiative. In a sense, whether Mrs Thatcher and her government were informed about the Belaúnde proposals before or after the sinking is largely irrelevant. In their book *The Sinking of the Belgrano*, Desmond Rice and Arthur Gavshon note: 'the indications suggest that Argentina was to be taught a lesson by the sternest military means, and the *General Belgrano* happened unfortunately to be the first target. To scupper the proposals, the British only had to say "No", and to pick on some point of real or imagined Argentine intransigence'.

But it was certainly not entirely Mrs Thatcher's war in another important respect. While the Prime Minister was determined that her role in the Falklands conflict should be seen as one of a noble and principled crusader, it is doubtful whether the task force would ever have succeeded without the intelligence and military support offered by Chile and, more controversially, by the US (see box).

Moreover, British priorities were not always what they seemed. Evidence has been provided elsewhere which suggests that the British government knew about Libya's arms sales to Argentina during the war, but decided that it would be convenient to turn a blind eye so as not to undermine its commercial interests in the Middle East. Equal or greater duplicity was shown by the British financial community. Fearful that tough action against the junta might jeopardise the City's reputation as a safe offshore island, the government displayed discreet flexibility in financial transactions involving Argentines and allowed the junta to open an escrow account in New York, into which interest due to British banks could be paid.

Jorge Luis Borges described the Falklands war as two bald men fighting over a comb. The war involved the death of over 1000 men, led by governments neither of which was, if the truth be told, primarily concerned about the right of 1800 British citizens to keep the government of their choice. In the process a peaceful island community was turned into a battleground.

If the task force had not been sent, it is possible to assume that the junta would have sought to perpetuate itself in power or, at the very least, to arrange a democracy suited to its own survival under another guise. A British defeat would almost certainly have inflated the Argentine military's self-image to the point of tempting it to achieve regional superiority. Other pending territorial disputes such as the Beagle Channel would also have evolved into bloody conflict.

If only out of a sense of self-esteem, no Argentine will admit in public a different version of history than that which pictures the collapse of the

The CIA: Mrs Thatcher's secret ally?

According to disclosures in Bob Woodward's book, *Veil: The Secret Wars of the CIA 1981–87*, the late CIA director, William Casey, played a central role in assisting Britain during the Falklands/Malvinas conflict. Woodward claims that Casey's commitment to the British cause was all the more effective because Jeanne Kirkpatrick, then US ambassador to the UN, had publicly declared support for Argentina, allegedly in return for the junta's backing of US policy in Central America. Argentina, writes Woodward, consequently deluded itself that the US was neutral. Instead, the CIA station chief in Buenos Aires and US military attaches were ordered to transmit all relevant information to London. The information received by MI6 was also routinely passed on to the White House and the State Department. Such was its quality, states the book, that officials from the Reagan administration were falling over each other to 'beat a path more quickly to the British'.

Casey's secret support for the Thatcher government was reportedly based on the fear that the Prime Minister was under severe political pressure and that her 'continuation in office hinged on the outcome of the war'. In return, the book suggests, a grateful Mrs Thatcher has been more than usually willing to assist the US in its foreign policy objectives, notably in the bombing of Libya and the minesweeping operation and military build-up in the Gulf.

Source: Guardian, 3 October 1987

Galtieri regime as born from its own contradictions and the awakening of the people's 'democratic spirit'. And yet it was the external reality of the Falklands war – deflating as it did Argentina's militarised political culture through the armed forces' humiliation on the battlefield – which was the real catalyst for change. Argentina's post-war trauma is partly explained by the fact that it owes the demise of General Galtieri to Mrs Thatcher.

The 'Falklands factor'

British policy towards the Falklands and Argentina since the war has been dominated, as it was during it, by Mrs Thatcher. The Prime Minister has shown herself not so much calculating as instinctive. It was the resolute approach which vindicated her in military and political terms. Hastings has described the Falklands as 'essentially a small colonial war midway in scale between a counter-insurgency operation and the armoured warfare seen in Europe in 1944–45'. And yet the mobilisation of the task force, the somewhat muddled campaign, and the ultimate courage and determination of professional soldiers to win through captured the imagination of the British public to the extent that other campaigns have done throughout history. There may have been immediate doubts raised in political and media circles and even among the soldiers themselves about whether the cause justified the cost, but there was popular enthusiasm for the achievements of the men and the iron lady who had guided them.

Not for the first nor for the last time, Thatcherism had caught a popular mood in Britain. The last opinion poll taken before the Argentine invasion showed that the Tory party was recovering its popularity from the low point it had reached the previous December. But Mrs Thatcher's handling of the Falklands war improved her standing even more. The Conservatives' rating rose from 34 per cent in March 1982 to a peak of 48 per cent when the war ended in June the same year. The Falklands factor may not have directly changed the attitudes of Labour party activists and their allies on the shop floor, the unemployed, and the poor inhabitants of Britain's inner cities, but it helped reinforce attitudes among those of the electorate who were already on the make well before Galtieri invaded the islands. It thus played a fundamental role in contributing to the Conservative victory in June 1983.

Post-war relations

In the immediate aftermath of the war, Mrs Thatcher's emotional attachment to the Falklands crisis and her myopic sense of policy were symbolised by her visit to the islands in January 1983 and by her habit of writing personal letters of support and condolence to the islanders and relatives of the war dead. 'My own memories of those days are still very much alive and will remain so', she wrote to John Smith, a member of the Falkland Islands Executive Council, in perhaps one of her most revealing personal statements:

> I will never forget the night when information came through that it looked as if the Argentine fleet was heading for the invasion of Port Stanley. I will never forget the day I smiled my way through constituency engagements in Finchley knowing that that night British troops would be making their landing in San Carlos. I was 8000 miles but only a heartbeat away from that silent armada, that hostile coast and those brave and loyal Islanders. Perhaps the proudest moment of my life was at 10 o'clock on the night of 14 June when I stood at the Despatch Box to announce that white flags were flying over Port Stanley.

Following the collapse of Galtieri and his succession by the 'transition' president General Reynaldo Bignone, Britain restored financial links with Argentina, but the move seemed less motivated by a desire to improve relations between the two countries than by a need to protect the City from the danger of a debt default. Similarly, the sending of a telegram congratulating Alfonsín on his inauguration was a Foreign Office initiative, extracted with great difficulty from Number Ten. The Argentine reply sent to Whitehall ended with the words 'where there is a will there is a way', but this, along with Alfonsín's statement in the *Observer* interview that he was prepared to consider a lease-back arrangement, was cold shouldered by London. In retrospect, one can only consider those first months of Alfonsín's government a tragic period of lost opportunity in the Falklands story.

In the figure of Alfonsín, the Argentines had voted in with a substantial majority the one politician who had not backed the invasion of the Falklands and who remained publicly committed to non-belligerence. Alfonsín's determination to eradicate the militarised political culture of his country was symbolised by his early overtures of peace to Chile over the Beagle Channel and his announcement that he was putting all the former juntas on trial for human rights violations. To have agreed to negotiate with Argentina then on an open agenda which included sovereignty (at a very much later stage) would not have been used by Alfonsín as a vindication of the junta's war, but as a signal that the rule of law and peaceful diplomacy produce more results in the community of nations than armed aggression.

And yet, in the months following his inauguration, Alfonsín received rather worse diplomatic treatment from Britain than that extended to successive military regimes by Labour and Conservative governments. Britain had excused the building of a new airport on the islands as essentially a political decision taken in the heat of the conflict, which was aimed principally at satisfying island opinion. But there was no effort, once Alfonsín had been inaugurated, to freeze the militarisation of the islands in symbolic response to Argentina's own forthright efforts to demilitarise. It is true that Argentina may have facilitated its case had it declared a de jure cessation of hostilities, but Alfonsín's public renunciation of the use of force over the islands could have been considered conciliatory enough to initiate at least talks about talks.

Mrs Thatcher's second term coincided with Alfonsín's first years in government. Britain's Conservative government was consolidating a political system with increasing self-assurance, while Argentina, on the other hand, had to endure the difficulties encountered by any nascent democracy emerging from many years of military rule. An acceptance that Britain could and should concede more lay behind the Foreign Office's so-called 'confidence building' measures. These included the relaxation of visa restrictions, the re-establishment of sporting and cultural links, and a tentative resumption of trade. At the same time, academics and parliamentarians from both countries, including Britain's antidote to the Falklands lobby – the South Atlantic Council – developed a two-track diplomacy aimed at getting round the absence of diplomatic ties through unofficial meetings.

Sovereignty: the stumbling block

Nevertheless the issue of sovereignty set in as an immovable obstacle in the way of a more genuine and wide-ranging reconciliation between the two countries. Mrs Thatcher's apparent contempt for Argentina's new democracy was stimulated by what she perceived as the essentially fragile and militaristic nature of the Alfonsín government, its determination to uphold Argentina's sovereignty claims, and in particular its deliberate attempts to split British public opinion by holding parallel diplomatic contacts with Neil Kinnock and David Steel. Both opposition leaders agreed that if elected to government they would initiate negotiations with Argentina on an open agenda which did not include sovereignty but did not preclude it either.

The contempt that Mrs Thatcher felt for what Argentina and its sympathisers described as a search for a 'negotiated settlement to the Falklands/Malvinas dispute' was reflected in her reaction to the United Nations General Assembly's overwhelming approval of a motion calling for 'negotiations on all aspects of the future of the islands'. Mrs Thatcher told the House of Commons on 28 November 1985: 'Anyone who thinks that a motion does not contain sovereignty must be absolutely bonkers'. She then repeated that sovereignty was non-negotiable.

Throughout the Falklands war Britain had shown itself more than willing to use the United Nations to condemn Argentine aggression conducted in the midst of negotiations. But now it had absolutely no desire even to contemplate the UN as an international agent of peace, to prevent any recurrence of conflict in the future, even though 107 countries, including the US, France, Italy, Greece, and Spain, approved the motion. (Only Oman, Belize and the Solomon Islands voted with Britain against).

Britain's attitude was all the more difficult to excuse given the fact that such a formula of compromise had been used by Lord Carrington in the Lisbon agreement of 1980 to overcome the initial stumbling block in the way of talks with the nascent democracy of Spain over the long-standing sovereignty dispute over Gibraltar. Mrs Thatcher had also agreed to talk to the Irish government personally about Ulster, while firmly denying that she was giving away anything on sovereignty.

Mrs Thatcher's refusal to consider sovereignty aborted the first and only post-war direct Anglo-Argentine talks in Berne in 1984. But Britain not only refused to talk about the issue; it also took steps to reinforce its rights to the islands. It granted kelpers full British nationality, formulated a new constitution for the islands, and in October 1986 declared its rights to a 200-mile fishing zone, declaring in the interim a conservation and management area within the 150-mile military protection zone already in place.

When Geoffrey Howe was asked by Eric Deakins MP how Britain could avoid an escalation of the dispute into another cod war, he replied: 'By a sensible response on the part of the Argentine government. If they were willing to respond to the moves that we have been pressing ahead with for some months and agreed to the establishment of a multilateral zone, which we regard as preferable, there would be no question of such a risk arising.'

The *Financial Times*, in an editorial at the time, argued that the entire basis of Argentine policy to the Falklands over the years has not been what Sir Geoffrey and his colleagues would call 'sensible'. 'We are now asked to believe that sense will emerge in Buenos Aires as a result of a British threat to use force, and possibly even the use of it.'

And yet the British government regarded itself as vindicated by subsequent events, fuelling the dangerous concept on which much of Mrs Thatcher's policy to the Falklands had been based: aggression does not pay, except when force is used by the British. In spite of some initial sabre-rattling by Argentina in the form of a rather exaggerated announcement that its troops were being mobilised in response to the new emergency of the fishing zone, it has since decided to opt for discreet contacts with the British through the mediation of the US. Although Britain was condemned at the UN for its move, and there was overwhelming diplomatic backing for Argentina, events on the ground showed up the duplicity of international diplomacy. Only the Soviet Union and Bulgaria signed separate fishing agreements with Argentina; all the other nations previously fishing in Falklands waters, including Argentina's 'supporters' such as Italy, Poland, and Spain, allowed their vessels to sign separate fishing agreements with the Falkland Islands government. In other words, Argentina's claim to the Falklands has not prevented commercial interests from pursuing a hard-headed course.

The other factor affecting the Argentine position has been Mrs Thatcher's election victory, which upset an Argentine strategy that since Berne had been pinned on a change of government.

Clearly, though, Mrs Thatcher can ill afford to be complacent about her Falklands record. The argument for negotiation on an open agenda still stands. For if Argentina were to continue to be treated by Britain no differently than it was under the military, there is no guarantee that the Malvinas will not provide the armed forces with the opportunity to bring the civilians to account and rehabilitate themselves in a war of revenge in which the political, economic, and human costs for both sides would certainly be much greater than in the last one.

Funding the fortress

An overview of the Falklands and the Thatcher years still gives the impression of rival and seemingly irreconcilable perceptions, in which two governments talk past each other rather than to each other. Britain's decision to turn the Falklands into the most sophisticated military base in the South Atlantic and to stimulate a symbiosis between the armed forces and the local population has only added to the problems.

According to the Ministry of Defence, up to the financial year 1985–6, the total costs of the Falklands campaign in 1982 and of the measures taken subsequently to ensure the defence of the islands amounted to some £2.6 billion. At their peak in 1982–3 and 1984–5, Falklands-attributable costs were equivalent to some 5 per cent and 4 per cent respectively of the total defence budget. Since 1984–5, Falklands costs have been declining. Public expenditure provision for 1987–8 is £257 million – equivalent to just under 1.4 per cent of the defence budget. The scale of the reduction, however, can only be properly seen in the wider context of the British economy and, in this sense, spending on the Falklands still seems disproportionate in comparison with what the government is prepared to invest in parts of Scotland and the inner cities.

'If it is considered necessary to maintain a sizeable garrison in the South Atlantic, we believe that force levels should be determined by operational need rather than by financial considerations. It would not be right to seek to defend the islands with resources insufficient to meet the actual or perceived threat', commented the House of Commons Defence Committee in its review of July 1987.

But the actual and perceived threat will always depend on the extent to which Britain and Argentina are prepared to negotiate on the future of the islands.

It is also difficult to isolate the islanders' own development from the demographic and political reality of neighbouring Argentina. Clearly there have been signs that with the increased fishing revenue and the investment and structural reforms undertaken since the end of the war, the islands have moved on from being a semi-feudal society to a more buoyant, if still dependent, community. When one prominent islander suggested publicly in summer 1987 that the islands should contemplate autonomy from Britain and negotiate directly with Argentina he was roundly attacked by his fellow kelpers.

And yet he seems to have gone to the crux of the problem. The islands' so-called development has so far been possible under British military protection. Thus there is no self-sufficiency, but only a more sophisticated form of dependency with continuing costs to the British taxpayer.

Chronology

1982

June	British forces recapture islands
July	Britain replaces 200-mile total exclusion zone with 150-mile protection zone, banning Argentine warships and military aircraft
	Mrs Thatcher reportedly furious at stance of peace and reconciliation adopted by Archbishop of Canterbury Robert Runcie in Falklands thanksgiving service at St Paul's
August	Argentine fishing vessels intercepted by British warships near islands; Argentina condemns an 'arrogant use of force'
October	US resumes arms sales to Argentina
November	UN votes overwhelmingly for Argentine resolution calling for renewed talks on dispute
December	Britain opposes sales of West German frigates to Argentina
	IMF aid package for Argentina of US$2.6 billion involves Lloyds Bank

1983

January   Bank of England refuses to participate in US$500-million loan to
                   Argentina as arranged by Bank for International Settlements in Basle
                   Mrs Thatcher pays surprise visit to Falklands
February   Defence of Falklands will cost every British taxpayer over £1,860
                   during next three years, according to official report
April   Britain prevents families of Argentine dead visiting Falklands graves
May   Foreign Secretary Sir Francis Pym adopts tough line over possible
                   negotiations with Argentina following his public interruption by Mrs
                   Thatcher at a press conference on the Falklands
June   Government announces that a strategic airfield, costing £215 million,
                   is to be built in the Falklands for completion in 1986
September   Britain tells UN Secretary General Pérez de Cuellar that it remains
                   opposed to negotiations over Falklands sovereignty

1984

August   Talks in Berne on restoring Anglo-Argentine relations collapse after
                   one day; Britain refuses to discuss sovereignty

1985

July   Britain lifts prohibition on Argentine imports, a move described in
                   Argentina as 'unilateral'
                   Commons Foreign Affairs Committee splits on party lines as to
                   whether the sinking of the *General Belgrano* outside the total
                   exclusion zone was justified or not
October   David Steel meets President Alfonsín and calls for immediate
                   negotiations on the Falklands, including sovereignty
November   UN General Assembly votes in favour of Anglo-Argentine talks to
                   cover all aspects of the Falklands dispute; Britain votes against

1986

August   Argentina claims that British military aircraft are guilty of aggression
                   towards Argentine fishing boats
October   Creation of 150-mile fisheries management and conservation zone
                   around Falklands
November   Britain rejects Argentine offer to end formal hostilities and
                   commence negotiations

1987

July   Britain announces purchase by Falklands Fisheries of £1-million
                   trawler to operate within fishing zone
                   Report of Commons Defence Committee assesses military campaign
                   of 1982
                   Falklands practically self-financing as result of the fishing zone
August   Mrs Thatcher delays the signing of a US$1.5-billion loan to Argentina
                   by British banks
                   Falklands Councillor Tony Blake calls for talks with Argentina and
                   increased autonomy for the islanders in a UN speech

Appendix 1: Arms sales to Latin America and the Caribbean, 1979–87

Argentina
1979	Lynx helicopters	8	Westland
1981	Blowpipe missiles	3	Shorts
1981	Tigercat land-based surface-to-air missiles	–	Shorts

Bahamas
1985	Protector class patrol boats	3	–

Barbados
1979	Fast attack craft	6	Brooke Marine
1980	Fast patrol boat	1	Brooke Marine

Belize
1982	BN-2A Defender transport planes	2	British Aerospace

Brazil
1980	Instruments for Xingu trainer planes	–	Smiths Industries
1981	Wasp helicopter	1	ex-Royal Navy
1981	Weapons control system for corvettes	–	Ferranti
1981	Spey engines for fighters	–	Rolls Royce
1981	Niteroi class frigate	1	–
1985	Sea Skua air-to-ship missiles	40	British Aerospace

Chile
1981	County class destroyer with Seacat missiles	2	ex-Royal Navy
1981	Canberra bomber/recce PR 57 planes	3	ex-RAF
1981	Hunter FGA-9 fighters	12	ex-RAF
1981	MM-38 Exocet ship-to-ship missiles	8	surplus stock
1981	Seacat ship-to-ship missiles	16	surplus stock
1981	Seacat ship-to-air missiles	8	surplus stock

Colombia
1980	HS748 2A transport aircraft	1	British Aerospace

Ecuador
1985	BAC-167 trainer/counter insurgency aircraft	6	British Aerospace

Guyana
1984	Skyvan-3M transport aircraft	1	–

Mexico
1980   BN-2A Islander transport aircraft   36   Britten Norman
1983   Azteca class patrol boats   5   –

St Vincent
1980   Fast patrol craft   1   Vosper Thorneycroft

Trinidad & Tobago
     Patrol boats   4   Souter & Sons

Source: Stockholm International Peace Research Institute (SIPRI).

Note 1: These sales represent only those worth more than £1 million.

Note 2: The dates refer to the year of order, not delivery.

Note 3: There are connections between the sale of weapons by other European countries and British engine suppliers. One example reveals how the Guatemalan air force uses the Netherlands-built Fokker VFW F-27 MK 400 (one was bought in 1984 and three in 1985), manufactured by a company which uses exclusively Rolls Royce engines. Furthermore, an increased UK involvement in arms deals with Brazil can be identified. Firstly, in 1982, the acquisition by Ferranti UK of 49 per cent ownership in Sistemas Ferranti do Brasil, in which IMBEC (a state body) has the majority holding, indicates a direct UK link in the production of naval electronics in that country. Secondly, the purchase by the RAF of an EMB-312 Brazilian Tucano to serve as its main trainer was part of a 'tit-for-tat' exchange, ensuring easier access to Brazilian arms manufacturers for UK component firms. Sales that have been facilitated include those involving parts for an AMX fighter and for the tank EET1 Osorio.

Source: Phil Evans, *British Arms Sales to Central America*, Central America Human Rights Committees, mimeo, London 1987.

Appendix 2: British aid to Latin America and the Caribbean, 1979—86

(£ thousands)

	1979	1980	1981	1982	1983	1984	1985	1986
Latin America								
Argentina	5	30	2	2	0	0	0	0
Belize	7172	4219	4781	2885	6098	5971	5706	3179
Bolivia	888	1158	1052	988	1199	1182	1421	1953
Brazil	888	1022	632	9960	5574	7780	4014	880
Chile	2131	2021	1452	675	442	257	334	373
Colombia	1242	848	765	617	635	460	838	1018
Costa Rica	623	606	570	486	1836	1666	12685	11538
Dom. Rep.	77	144	139	139	176	61	24	42
Ecuador	1897	945	762	1046	783	916	909	836
El Salvador	448	265	41	13	0	205	103	239
Falklands	915	1015	1058	4025	9053	6016	10700	10252
Guatemala	14	35	15	4	0	0	7	10
Haiti	5	24	4	1	19	8	3	331
Honduras	230	335	5002	2272	6670	3446	3653	1258
Mexico	1186	1577	1464	34334	2827	517	773	803
Nicaragua	246	127	91	49	64	9	116	86
Panama	63	94	102	62	43	49	67	70
Paraguay	267	270	219	3263	1281	207	51	221
Peru	882	950	973	676	4427	476	928	1214
Uruguay	35	37	9	11	16	14	7	13
Venezuela	0	0	0	2	3	0	1	10

(£ thousands)

	1979	1980	1981	1982	1983	1984	1985	1986
Caribbean								
Anguilla	1060	991	1296	1059	1426	1026	1086	1589
Antigua &								
Barbuda	778	485	939	524	427	422	544	767
Bahamas	65	70	41	17	4	7	8	7
Barbados	710	620	3575	2502	422	338	298	442
Bermuda	15	28	12	0	33	17	17	30
British								
Virgin Is.	781	1232	1241	1471	1161	718	1172	831
Cayman Is.	283	443	199	34	2	0	470	1649
Dominica	2864	2536	1575	1934	1664	1216	1600	2337
Grenada	252	259	83	78	85	693	1450	776
Guyana	2606	2356	2475	1724	1555	419	354	487
Jamaica	6369	4767	8681	8868	8922	15243	7986	3777
Monserrat	528	1222	1127	1823	1041	1268	1223	2015
St Kitts-Nevis	686	777	575	858	821	922	918	954
St Lucia	844	1233	2201	1559	2630	475	530	758
St Vincent	2526	819	1349	1154	660	582	1250	857
Trinidad &								
Tobago	149	171	93	65	57	29	136	61
Turks &								
Caicos Is.	1015	1261	3362	5716	4217	3923	3588	5387

Source: Overseas Development Administration, *British Aid Statistics*, 1976–80, 1981–5, 1982–6.

Note: These figures include technical co-operation (personnel overseas, education and training, research and training, surveys, consultancies, equipment and supplies, pensions and compensation, grants to voluntary organisations).

Organisations working on Latin America and the Caribbean

Committee for Human Rights in Argentina, Latin American House, Kingsgate Place, London NW6 4TA.

Britain-Cuba Resource Centre, Latin American House, Kingsgate Place, London NW6 4TA.

Caribbean Labour Solidarity, 138 Southgate Road, London N1.

Caribbean Resource Centre, 5 Westminster Bridge Road, London SE1.

Carila Latin American Resource Centre, 29 Islington Park Street, London N1 1QB.

Chile Committee for Human Rights, 13–16 Borough Road, London SE1 0AL.

Chile Democratico, 95–97 Old Street, London EC1V 1QB.

Chile Solidarity Campaign, 129 Seven Sisters Road, London N7.

Colombian Committee for Human Rights, 29 Islington Park Street, London N1 1QB.

Colombian Solidarity Committee, Latin American House, Kingsgate Place, London NW6 4TA.

El Salvador Committee for Human Rights, 83 Margaret Street, London W1N 7HB.

El Salvador Solidarity Campaign, 13–16 Borough Road, London SE1 0AL.

Guatemala Committee for Human Rights, 83 Margaret Street, London W1N 7HB.

Guatemala Working Group, c/o LAB, 1 Amwell Street, London EC1R 1UL.

Trade Union Support for Guatemala, 29 Islington Park Street, London N1 1QB.

Honduras Committee for Human Rights, Latin American House, Kingsgate Place, London NW6 4TA.

Nicaragua Solidarity Campaign, 23 Bevenden Street, London N1 6BH.

Paraguay Committee for Human Rights, Latin American House, Kingsgate Place, London NW6 4TA.

Peru Support Group, Latin American House, Kingsgate Place, London NW6 4TA.

Puerto Rico Support Committee, Latin American House, Kingsgate Place, London NW6 4TA.

New LAB books

The Great Tin Crash: Bolivia and the World Tin Market

Tells the story of tin; from the rise of the tin can to the collapse of the world tin market in October 1985, and its impact on the mineworkers and their families in Bolivia.

'We recommend it to be read by all mineworkers unions.' Miners International Federation.

Price £3.70

Green Gold: Bananas and Dependency in the Eastern Caribbean

Looks at the history, recent developments and future prospects for the banana industry in Dominica, Grenada, St Lucia and St Vincent, focusing on conditions for the region's small farmers.

Price £4.70

Guatemala: False Hope, False Freedom

Draws upon recent research in Guatemala by the author, James Painter, to examine the enduring chasm between the rich and the poor, the continued counter-insurgency campaign, and the policies of President Cerezo's Christian Democrat party.

Published jointly with the Catholic Institute for International Relations.

Price £5.50

Soft Drink, Hard Labour: Guatemalan Workers Take on Coca-Cola
Miguel Angel Reyes and Mike Gatehouse

Covers the recent history of the struggle of the Coca-Cola workers in Guatemala against their management, including the 1984 occupation, the general political and trade union context behind it, and Coca-Cola's local and international response to it.

Price £1.50

Prices include post and packing

For a complete list of LAB books write to LAB, 1 Amwell Street, London EC1R 1UL.

THE EUROPEAN CHALLENGE

The Falklands war has substantially changed Britain's relations with Latin America, and raises yet again the question of Europe's role in the continent. Prior to the war, Western Europe had distanced itself in numerous ways from the polices of the United States in the region, particularly with respect to the crisis in Central America.

Many observers welcomed the breach in the long-standing alliance between Europe and the United States and saw European involvement in Latin America as a counterweight to the region's traditional dependence on the US. They viewed Europe as a potential ally whose greater concern with North-South issues rather than the East-West conflict could benefit the region.

The Falklands crisis illustrated that the breach was not as wide as many imagined, and that the North-South dimension of the problem was exacerbated rather than resolved sympathetically by Europe's actions.

The European Challenge sets out to explore various aspects of Europe's relations with Latin America: transnational investment, the role of the EEC, financial flows, European social democracy, human rights and arms sales. Through an analysis of the political and economic interests behind the European challenge, the book questions whether Europe can be expected to promote the kind of development in Latin America which will advance the cause of social and economic justice in the region. In the wake of the South Atlantic crisis it is particularly relevant to all those who seek to build bridges with Latin America.

Latin America Bureau

£3.95 plus £0.75 postage and packing
US$8.00 plus US$3.00 postage and packing
ISBN 0 906156 14 9   244pp

Available from **Latin America Bureau, 1 Amwell Street, London EC1R 1UL**

Other LAB publications

Paraguay: Power Game
September 1980. 76pp. £1.50

**Under the Eagle: US Intervention in Central America
and the Caribbean**
by Jenny Pearce
Updated edition April 1982. 295pp. £5.95

**The European Challenge: Europe's New
Role in Latin America**
June 1982. 244pp. £3.95

Guyana: Fraudulent Revolution
March 1984. 106pp. £3.50

Grenada: Whose Freedom?
by Fitzroy Ambursley and James Dunkerley
April 1984. 128pp. £3.50

Peru: Paths to Poverty
by Michael Reid
February 1985. 136pp. £3.50

Haiti: Family Business
by Rod Prince
September 1985. 86pp. £3.50

Honduras: State for Sale
by Richard Lapper and James Painter
November 1985. 132pp. £3.50

**Promised Land: Peasant Rebellion in Chalatenango,
El Salvador**
by Jenny Pearce
March 1986. 320pp. £6.95

Prices do not include postage

Latin America Bureau

The Latin America Bureau is a small, independent, non-profit making research organisation established in 1977. LAB is concerned with human rights and related social, political and economic issues in Central and South America and the Caribbean. We carry out research and publish books, publicise and lobby on these issues and establish support links with Latin American groups. We also brief the media, organise seminars and have a growing programme of schools publications.